I SAILED WITH RASMUSSEN

Knud Rasmussen.

I SAILED WITH RASMUSSEN

by
PETER FREUCHEN

JULIAN MESSNER, INC.   NEW YORK, N. Y.

Published by Julian Messner, Inc.
8 West 40 Street, New York 18

Published simultaneously in Canada
by The Copp Clark Publishing Co. Limited

Copyright © 1958 by Julian Messner, Inc.

Printed in the United States of America

*Some of the incidents described in this book
were told in Peter Freuchen's* Arctic Adventure.

Library of Congress Catalog Card No. 58-11842

To Hanne and Inge and

Niels Christian

from their

Godfather

ILLUSTRATIONS

FOREWORD

~~~~~~

This book is not intended to be, nor does it claim to be, an exhaustive scholarly work about Knud Rasmussen. Such a work will be produced by others; his name will never be forgotten in Denmark's history.

I only want to try to give an impression of the friend of my youth and the companion of my manhood, of the man who has meant most to me in this world.

And that I can probably do best by telling what I know about him.

Behind his fame, Knud Rasmussen was a vitally live man, a human being who loved life. He cherished human beings, and made a festive occasion out of every moment which was beyond others' ability to make it so.

As a youth he had fought his way forward, not only through snow and ice, but through the crowds of men to reach the heights. Life in the polar regions hardened him, and he turned the monotony of the long winter night to useful pursuits and achievement.

For many years I traveled around in these regions with Knud Rasmussen. Nothing draws men closer than to hunger together, to see death in each other's eyes. I knew him as did no one else. Lying together in snow huts during snowstorms of many days' duration, waiting for better weather, and seeking to drown our hunger by each telling the other everything he knows—then you pour out your life, and old memories emerge in your mind. The old boyhood experiences become alive again, and your innermost thoughts and hopes find expression.

That is how I know things about Knud Rasmussen that no one else knows, and that is what I want to write about.

The spirited, energetic, joyous Knud Rasmussen—this is the man I want to tell about. Historians can render critical accounts of his scientific achievements and appraise his place in the stormy world. I just want to remember and to write things down. I have heard about his childhood from his own lips. I saw much of him during the years of his youth; the rest he told me about as we lay imprisoned in the snow huts. I had a part in the development of his manhood through the exciting and challenging times when plans were born, before they became realities, and later, through the deeds of now bygone days.

We never separated; in later years we each simply went our own way, where we thought we could function most usefully alone. Oh, how I missed him!

I am one of those who believes in progress and development in life. I believe in human happiness, and I have seen that it thrives among the white races and cultivated peoples beter than among primitive peoples. This I learned from Knud Rasmussen; however, if we had believed that we took something from the Eskimos among whom we lived without giving them more in return for what they lost, we would not have been honest. We would have felt like thieves and exploiters of their beautiful, clean spirit and way of life.

Knud Rasmussen, throughout his whole life, left the people he visited richer than when he came to them; thus he earned the inalienable right to be the happy and whole man that he was.

Peter Freuchen

Greenland Sea
DENMARK HARBOR
PUSTERVIG
CAPE RIGSDAGEN
DENMARK FJORD
INDEPENDENCE FJORD
MYLIUS-ERICHSEN LAND
PEARY LAND
NAVY CLIFF
FREUCHEN LAND
GREENLAND
WARMING LAND
NYBOE LAND
GRANT LAND
HUMBOLDT GLACIER
GRINNELL LAND
CAPE SEDDON
ITUISALIK
TASSIUSSAK
THOM I.
BRYANT I.
MELVILLE BAY
NUGSSUAQ
BJOERNEBORG
UPERNIVIK
PROEVEN
ETAH
NEQE
THULE
BUSHNAN I.
CAPE YORK
PARKER SNOW BAY
SAUNDER'S I.
HAKLUYT ISLAND
NORTHUMBERLAND ISLAND
ELLESMERE Land
Baffin Bay

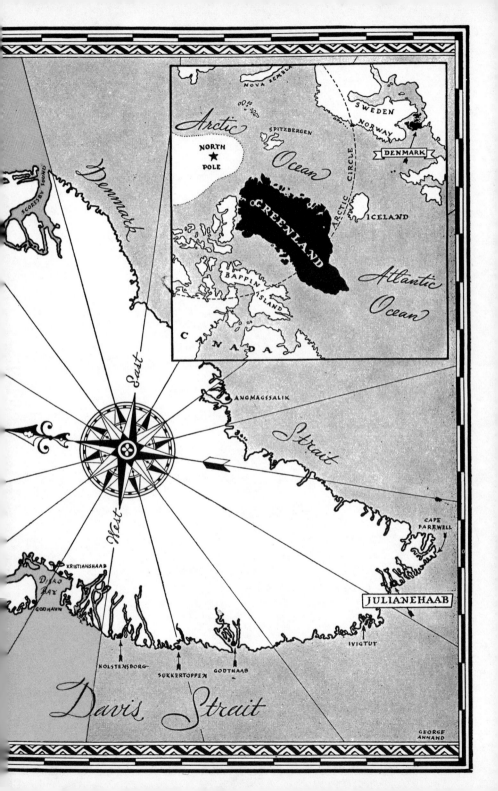

I first met Knud Rasmussen in 1909 when I was twenty-five years old. Three years earlier, I had come to the conclusion that I was not cut out to be a doctor and had quit the Medical School at the University of Copenhagen.

At the time I left the University, an expedition was being organized, financed by the Danish government and private funds, to map the northeastern part of Greenland, which had not yet been explored. I decided to offer my services and at first was refused. But finally the authorities promised me a berth, and we sailed out of Copenhagen in June of that year.

The expedition lasted three years and when we finally returned, our reception at Copenhagen was tremendous. The King, the Prime Minister, the heads of the University and great crowds of people were there to greet us. For days there were lavish banquets in our honor and countless interviews by the press. But soon there came a day when we were no longer news.

I went back to the University and took up chemistry and surveying. I found it difficult to concentrate on my studies and almost impossible to accept my classmates as equals—they understood nothing but school pastimes and pleasures, I felt, whereas I, Peter Freuchen, was an Arctic explorer!

It was through some of the men who had been with me on the expedition that I met Knud. He soon became my closest friend and changed the entire course of my life.

Knud was a remarkable lad who was born in June of 1879 at the parsonage of Jakobshavn, a Danish settlement on the west coast of Greenland along Disko Bay.

His father, Pastor Christian Rasmussen, was a Danish missionary who lived in Greenland for twenty-eight years. His district included the entire northern half of colonized Greenland, which extended about two-thirds of the way up the west coast. There he was well known for his extensive dog sled travels. At one time he had five parishes simultaneously, and the entire winter he would travel around on dog sled to preach and minister to his people, most of whom were Greenlanders, as Eskimos with Danish blood are called. Loved by all and known throughout all North Greenland, he was in no way a lesser man than his subsequently famous son insofar as strength and hardiness and venturesomeness were concerned.

Knud's mother was part Eskimo. Her father was a unique personality. His name was Knud Fleischer, and he was born in Greenland of Norwegian parents. He became a colonial administrator and a very prosperous man. He married a penniless orphaned girl, a heathen Eskimo, whom he had found close to starvation during

16

Peter Freuchen—Arctic explorer!

a famine in Christianshaab on Disko Bay. She was given baptism and an education, and she later developed into a richly endowed human being.

Knud early developed an independent view of things around him, and a will that was not easily bent. When it was time for him to get up in the morning, it was often hard to get him to finish dressing. He had so many things that were more important to take care of that his nurse-maid and Aunt Helga, his mother's sister, had their troubles in getting him ready for the morning devotion in the parlor.

"Please put your stocking on, Little Knud," the nurse-maid would plead. Then Aunt Helga would speak more firmly. But it didn't help.

First he had to take a look at Disko Island, the largest island off the west coast of Greenland, which lay craggy and beautifully sun-lit out there in the sea. In addition there were always icebergs from the great glacier nearby. They were fascinating things. Where did they come from; where did they sail to? He demanded answers, and he was told many strange tales. And all this had to be done before his stocking was pulled up to his knee.

If a hunter came sailing by, it occupied his whole attention. It was much more fun to watch him paddling his kayak than to get washed and dressed.

Though Knud was the eldest of the Rasmussen children, he was more difficult to manage than either his sister, May, or his little brother, Christian.

Few did as much for the pastor's children as Aunt Helga, and they loved her with all their hearts. Still they plagued her with tricks and childish pranks. Aunt Helga lived with the family and taught the children. She kept house with her mother in the lower story of the parsonage, and there she held her classes.

Knud was a difficult pupil. He decided that he would recite his lesson only while lying on his stomach across a chair. He was prepared to study geography, but only if he could sit under the table. One day he failed to show up, and Aunt Helga had to go out and look for him. That was such fun that he made it a rule to hide in the coal bin or the doghouse or some other place so that the family had to come out and find him if they wanted him to attend classes.

But after a while things went too far, and one fine day Aunt Helga announced that she wasn't going to teach them any longer. The thing was that the two younger children looked up to Knud in everything and began to ape his ways. Aunt Helga jumped up on a rock outside the house and told them that since they wouldn't be decent and well-behaved school children she would retire to the mountains and become a mountain phantom; this was one of the most horrible things that could happen in Greenland.

The children then ran weeping after her and implored her to come back; "No, no, Auntie, come back. We promise to be good and to study as we should."

Knud later told me about his fear of losing his aunt at that time; it was one of the unhappiest days of his childhood.

At that time in Knud's life, the man he idolized most in the world was his father's dog trainer, whose name was Godman. Godman also acted as navigator and despotic captain of the large boat in which the pastor made his annual summer trip throughout his district, which covered a distance of more than twelve hundred miles.

Knud often told me about this man, who made his first whip for him, and who took him along on sled journeys. When he was about six years old he decided: "I want to be like him when I get big."

It was natural that a boy like Knud should become the leader of his companions. And this he was from the earliest days.

His later colleagues in Thule, Seckman Rosback and Enok Kristiansen, two Greenlanders, once told me that their childhood's happiest times were their days of playing with Knud. He always wanted to play at exploration and expeditions. They were his dogs, and he fed them bread. Seckman has told of how Knud tied them up, because that was part of the game, and left them tied up while he went to get bread from his mother. Once Knud was kept from returning right away, being drafted to perform some chore or other about the house, and Seckman did not dare untie himself and go home, but remained standing and waited for many hours.

A happy childhood. A mother so tender and good as but few have been. There were three children in the family, but Mrs. Rasmussen took care of others. When her daughter May was born, there was in the colony a poor little Eskimo girl whose mother had died. There is no such thing as a dairy in Greenland. It meant almost certain death for a child to lose its mother. But the pastor's wife laid the little girl to her breast and divided her milk between the poor child and her own daughter.

20

One night during the cold season, many years later, we were stranded in the Upernavik district on the west coast along Baffin Bay. Knud's mother had recently died, and he talked for hours about her faith in him and in the good that exists in the world. A mother who had never demanded, who had always given. We sat and froze in a hut, but there a son delivered a eulogy to his mother, and a more beautiful one has never been given in this world.

Pastor Rasmussen was not only a traveling dispenser of God's grace; he was a linguist of high rank, and his scholarly works had many important results, primarily the invaluable Greenlandic grammar and the comprehensive Greenlandic dictionary which he issued. Later he became a lecturer in Greenlandic in Copenhagen after having moved to Denmark. Knud inherited his father's facility for languages. Perhaps it was a kind of musical sense that fixed words in his brain much as a blotter soaks up ink.

From the time Knud was a small child he was free to come and go in all the Eskimo households. The old women always had a piece of sugar-candy to take with their coffee, and the pastor's little boy was welcomed by all of them. His disposition was always good, and he never came without bearing a gift, often of a loaf of rye bread or perhaps only a pretty stone that he had found. I have known people to keep such stones as amulets; they were gifts from "Little Knud," which no one could pry loose from their owners.

Knud was fascinated by the very old women in Jakobshavn. These old women told him strange and remarkable tales of the pure Eskimos living far up north beyond the

Danish colony in territory where few people had dared to venture. It was said that they were wild killers and that they dressed in bearskins and killed whales. Many mysterious things were told of these northerners. No one knew anything for sure, and everyone added something from his own fantasy. This never frightened Knud. He wanted to go there when he grew up, he said.

Then, to show him how foolish his childish notion was, they told him how Eskimos had treated a small band of Greenlanders, who years before had undertaken a journey to the far north.

They had coaxed the Greenlanders up on a cliff and then pulled down the ropes they had climbed up on. The fear-struck guests remained wailing up on the heights for four days. At last despair drove them to try climbing down the steep cliffside. They finally made it, but they never ventured north again.

The north was also a place of dismal darkness, they said, but nothing frightened Knud. He continued to insist that he wanted to go up there; his father had promised him some dogs soon, and when they became big and strong he would drive on up. The women laughed, but Knud never forgot something he had resolved upon.

One of the events of Knud's childhood that probably had much to do with his later career was Fridtjof Nansen's daring exploit. In 1888 Nansen, a young, unknown Norwegian, and five companions attempted the first complete crossing of Greenland's inland ice, working from east to west. It was expected that Nansen would eventually reach Disko Bay. It was Nansen's companions, said to be Lapps, that most interested Knud and his young friend Jörgen

Brönlund. They sat and talked about these Lapps end-lessly. Knud had picked up from time to time a word or two about Laplanders from the conversation of the grown-ups, and from this scanty knowledge the two boys impro-vised further.

The *Greenland Commercial* had offered a prize of twenty crowns to the first person to sight Nansen, and Mr. Olsen, the administrator of Akugdlit, one of the nearby districts, had offered from his own pocket two hundred crowns, a huge sum.

Greatly excited by such a prize, Knud and Jörgen Brön-lund set out one summer evening when it was very light. They walked and talked until finally they got so far that they could no longer see the mountain near their settle-ment. Soon they became worried, but still they went on, until they reached a high point from which they could look out over a great stretch.

Then Knud realized that he could see as far as he would be able to walk, so it was no use to try any longer. And since the weariness in his legs and the hunger in his stomach had asserted themselves more strongly than the desire for the two hundred crowns, which he had mes-merized himself into trying for, he came home.

Not long afterwards, a real adventure came Knud's way. A painter named Riis Carstensen, whose travels had taken him far around the world, came to Greenland, which at that time seldom saw any strangers and hardly any artists. Knud drank in his stories and looked at the pictures he had brought with him from the tropics, and he thought he had met the greatest man in the world. It seemed to the boy that from now on his games and his dreams would take a different direction.

Riis Carstensen decided to set out on an expedition to the Northeast Bay region just at the time that Pastor Rasmussen was about to leave on his summer trip. This time, Knud was to go along. He and his father would accompany Riis Carstensen up to the northern part of Disko Bay.

On the way they stopped to visit Knud's Uncle Carl Fleischer who was the administrator of the outpost maintained by the Danish government at Qeqertak, in the Torssukátak Fjord. He was married to a wonderful woman, a Greenlander, Aunt Augustine, who was a hostess without equal. Her handiwork in the preparation of skins was famed and unexcelled, and she always had stores of warm clothing on hand for the Rasmussen children when they came on visits.

This trip was paradise for Knud.

The people in Qeqertak filled Knud's head with remarkable things. These were people who lived very isolated lives and had strange imaginations. The dismal rumbling of the enormous icebergs that steadily fell out of the glaciers and the winter darkness nourished their fantasies.

They told Knud about a man who had taken to the mountains to become a phantom. People who abandoned the society of other people were given the name *qivitok*. It was thought that because they separated themselves so far from the church and could not hear the Word of God they were sought out and possessed by the devil. In reality it was most often feeble-minded persons who took to the mountains, and therefore they were unable to come back again. They were shot at if they approached dwellings.

An old woman told Knud about a man whom she had known a few years before. The unfortunate man had lost his children when an iceberg had plunged down upon the boat in which they were rowing. The same summer he had taken to the mountains and wandered about. Ten days later he was found dead; his face was already covered with black hairs and one of his feet had begun to wither, taking on the appearance of a reindeer hoof.

On the way home, Knud and his father met Deputy Majgaard, who had spent the year before with Peary, the subsequent discoverer of the North Pole. They had traveled inland over the ice, and Majgaard therefore knew at first hand of conditions to be found there.

Knud's expedition fever was now fanned again. Majgaard's accounts and his opinion that Nansen's expedition had a good chance of success caused the boy to forget the Eskimos and their stories for a while. He sat and dreamed about journeys across the endless, white snow fields.

But it was best of all back home in Jakobshavn. The games never stopped. Greenlander boys have the advantage over Danish boys insofar as their games are the same as their later occupation. Miniature hunting equipment is given to Greenlanders as soon as they can walk; as they get bigger their toys merely get bigger and bigger.

Knud was brought up in this way, with one major exception: he never got a kayak as a little boy. On this point, his father was unbending, and Knud often told me that he was somewhat lacking in kayak-handling because his father had failed to give him a child's kayak when he was six years old.

Life in Greenland during Knud Rasmussen's boyhood was static. Those were the days of the sailing ships. These beautiful ships, brig or bark, made but one or two trips in a year. Often they wintered in Greenland and their arrival in a colony was a festive occasion to which the Danish children no less than the Eskimos looked longingly forward. As soon as the ice began to break up they started to talk about it, and Disko Bay, which was full of icebergs, fed the imagination endlessly. An iceberg far out could resemble all kinds of remarkable things and most of all a sailing ship. How often the children stood and looked out the windows, waiting to see a ship steering in toward the inlet!

In the colony there were prizes for those who first sighted the ship, and loud cries would proclaim through the whole colony that now the ship was there, the big event of the summer. Jubilation and joy for everyone.

When finally the wind had brought the ship so near land that the colonial governor thought it proper, the colony's rowing sloops were sent to help with the berthing. Then the children were taken along, and it was a great joy for Knud to come along in the boat, to row and feel that he was one of those who tugged at the oars and helped bring the enormous ship into port.

But it sometimes happened that the ship arrived during rain and sleet, which made it quite invisible; once, no one realized that the ship was coming before it loomed up right outside the harbor and surprised them all. That was one of the happenings that remained clear in Knud's memory for many years. The captain seemed to him to be some kind of conjurer in the way he guided his ship in past the many icebergs and through the difficult coastal waters.

The ships that came always brought mysterious packages from Denmark. The children got a lot of them at once, of course, but with a very secretive look Knud's mother would sort out some from the rest and put them away until Christmas. These packages, which were kept in a large cupboard, were always interesting and provided an everlasting topic of conversation.

Some of Knud's best friends lived in the little settlement of Igdlumiut, a few miles from Jakobshavn proper. Knud would sometimes seek comfort with them when he thought that the discipline at home got a little too strict and when the impossible was demanded, such as keeping fixed hours for meals and other things that didn't quite suit him. He much preferred to lie in a boat out on the sea and fish for polar cod or to run behind dog sleds in the winter.

Many years later I often got annoyed at the numbers of young folks who would always hang onto the uprights of the sled and drag behind when it departed from a settlement, and I often wondered why Knud, who was so solicitous about his dogs, allowed the children to hang on, forming a long human tail, thus cutting down the speed and tiring the dogs.

"Oh," said Knud, "you don't know what a thrill it was for me to hang onto the sleds and run after them far over the harbor when the sleds back home in Jakobshavn took off in the winter. We ran and ran, and then we would

27

decide to go back, but we would run still farther, and when we got back we bragged to each other about how far we had gone. Yes, it is often tiring to have them hanging on, but you haven't known the joy we boys felt when we got back after having been so far afield."

One of Knud's vivid childhood memories was to see the hunters of the district come home with their sleds loaded with blubber and the wonderful whaleskin, *mattak,* which is not only the tenderest delicacy one can imagine, but which also serves to mark in a festive way the end of the hungry days, when starvation has been held at bay with frog and shark meat, something one eats only when all other supplies are gone. Ordinarily, the meat of sharks was used for dog food and was excellent for that.

In Eskimo society that meat which is brought in from the sea is common property. The harpooner has the right to only a small part. The rest is divided up by the community. The rules differ a little from place to place, and in Jakobshavn every man could plunge his knife into the carcass and carve out huge chunks of meat, as much as he could get. The harpooners took theirs first, and then the men, women, and children would take over, like wild dogs attacking a quarry. This was the right of everyone, and to the excitement of getting the meat and blubber and *mattak* was added the spice of competing to see who could flense out the biggest piece.

Knud took part in these feasts. This probably did not have his mother's approval, but he naturally forgot about that; and when he came home with his clothing stained with fat and blood and his hands and face dirty and smeared, his parents were usually understanding about it.

During such feasts there is much story-telling. Every locality has its legends, folk songs, and stories of strange things that happened right there. At Sermeriut there was a ravine in the cliff into which would be thrown witches, old, sick, and weak people who had become a burden, and infants who had lost their parents. The old women would tell of this by the hour and Knud's imagination was set afire by these tales. He remembered that his own grandmother had been an orphaned heathen child. Once he thought about this so hard that he darted from the company and ran home alone in the dark.

He rushed in to his Aunt Helga and told her that he would stay at home with his mother and father and aunt and that nobody was going to throw them down the ravine. Such a hysterical attack, about which he told me himself, was quite unusual in that healthy and active boy. But it shows that the power of his imagination was already great and violent.

When summer drew to a close and the storms of autumn began to blow, the colony would begin its preparations to defy the winter. The large boats were drawn up on land. The time for sailing was past.

At this time of year, nothing interested Knud more than watching the ice get thicker and thicker as the days went by. Once his parents saw him inch his way out on the thin ice to find out if it was strong enough. Then a prohibition was proclaimed and an oath was demanded of him that he would not go out on the ice. If he failed to respect his oath he would not be allowed to leave the garden. He soon learned that so long as the ice on the sea is

29

black one must not trust it; only after it has changed to a milky-gray color is it safe.

When the ice was safe Knud was allowed to drive his little sled over the land and out over the ice. He had never really needed any instruction in driving a sled. It came naturally; dog driving is an inborn skill, and one cannot learn it. It is not the whip, not force alone that counts; it is an intimate understanding of the nature of the dogs. He could always get his dogs to persevere, to do what they had to do, no matter how exhausted they were. When, finally, a dog in Knud's team laid himself down, it was death that had defeated him, not the whip. Knud had the gift of being able to hypnotize his dogs so that they gave to the limit of their strength, even if they were in the lead, and so made it easier for the dogs behind.

At Christmas time the Greenlanders followed the old custom of going around and singing outside the houses. The Christmas holidays were spent in festive visits back and forth with the many friends of the family. There was dancing in the cooper's shop, when the cold outside was thirty or forty below; everyone had to maintain his own warmth through constant dancing and movement. There would be a great deal of laughter and horseplay and general merriment. It was quite different from the dancing in the summer, when the sailors and the ship season set their stamp on the scene and the mood.

At carnival time the children dressed themselves in the most fantastic costumes, wandered around from house to house, enacted comedy, and played a lot of merry pranks. At such times Knud was among the most ardent. He was a clown whose antics and humor never failed to thaw the sourest nature. There are still some old people living who remember his pranks as a boy and who remember his ringing shouts, when he laughed so heartily that everybody became good-humored just listening.

But there were also many times of hardship. At such times Knud learned to hold the Eskimos dear, and they him. The kitchen door of the parsonage was always open. Children came in to eat, women to visit. They knew that there was always coffee in the pot, and that there was always a piece of rye bread for them to take home. It is true that these times cost the pastor quite a bit of money, but for it he won the confidence and affection of these people, which is one of the greatest things one can have. The pastor and his wife taught their children well to note and remember the uncertainty of man's material lot on earth.

A Greenland childhood was indeed a paradise for a young, active, and healthy boy like Knud. Life in the open, which toughened him for his struggle against the hardships of nature in the years ahead; knowledge of the people and the conditions in which he was to live his entire life; and affection for those people, who gave to him of that goodness which he himself felt; all this became for Knud the force which formed his mind and built his strength.

~~~~~~

But a day came when this happy existence drew to an end. The voyage to Denmark had always loomed in the distance, half-threatening, half-beguiling. It had always seemed dreamlike, though, and when Knud actually saw the mountains disappear and the icebergs in the ocean become fewer and fewer, he experienced his first real loneliness.

Until then his life had been without troubles, an endless party, and at home he had experienced only affection and peacefulness. His father had taken over his education from Aunt Helga during recent years. From him Knud learned many things, and already knew some Latin and Greek.

It had been decided that he would enter the Herlufsholm school for boys in Denmark. His father had gone to school there, and the happiest memories of the pastor's youth were the days he spent there. When Knud was homesick for Jakobshavn's ice mountains during the voyage to Denmark, his father told him of the joys that lay before him when he would don his student's uniform and sleep in the historic old hall at the school.

Knud told me all about this once when we were weatherbound in Thule. It was his life's first defeat: He was not accepted at the school at Herlufsholm.

With happy anticipation, he had accompanied his father on the two-hour train ride from Copenhagen to Herlufsholm. His father had been in a jolly mood and told him of things he remembered from his schooldays. He was so pleased that his boy was to relive *his* experiences, and that he would be able to hear about them all over again.

But when Knud took the examination, he failed. They didn't want him as a student.

Knud remembered the walk from the school to the railroad station for the rest of his life. Back through the woods they came without speaking. Both were crushed, and involuntarily Knud's hand sought his father's as if to offer consolation.

Then his father began to talk to him in the most endearing voice a father could have:

"You mustn't feel bad about this, Little Knud; after all, there are many other schools, and it might well be that you wouldn't have liked it here at all! It is not you who should feel bad about it. You'll certainly do all right for yourself. It was my failure; it was I who didn't measure up. I obviously have not taught you as well as I should have. No, it's my fault, and it is only I who should be sad, because I am the one who has not done his job well enough."

And Knud felt his father's affection so strongly at that

moment that he never forgot the walk with his father as long as he lived. Up to then nothing had ever gotten in his way. He had been lovingly spoiled at home, favored by the Greenlanders, and richly endowed with natural gifts, none of which had ever taught him anything about the need for struggle and systematic work in order to attain something. Well, he was after all only a boy, and his schooling was now to take place in Copenhagen.

Let it be said right here and now that Knud, who became a Danish national hero, who received more scientific honors than any other contemporary Dane, was not a particularly good student. He did not shine in diligence or in scholarly achievement, but he was highly regarded and admired by his schoolmates, and most of his teachers loved him for the rest of their lives.

I myself did not know him during his school years. He lived in the home of Mr. Jörgensen, a wine dealer. The old wine merchant understood the peculiarities in the boy's character and guided him accordingly.

Knud did not always have it easy in school. There were some teachers who misinterpreted their functions.

Though Knud had a great deal of talent for languages, mathematics did not come easily to him, as is true of many Greenlanders; and that is probably the reason that his father did not stress this subject sufficiently in his instruction. It was primarily in this subject that he failed in his entrance examinations at Herlufsholm.

During his earliest schooldays in Copenhagen, Knud had a teacher in arithmetic who was unsympathetic and pedantic. He was one of those teachers, occasionally to be found, who takes pleasure out of playing the great man in front of a classroom of boys, who, because of their youth and their positions as pupils, have neither the power nor the right to retaliate. This incompetent teacher used to send Knud up to the big blackboard and have him work out his problems in front of the class. He never corrected him, but let him go on no matter how wrong the solution might be. When the boy finally came to a dead end and had wandered into completely impossible figures and formulas, the teacher would begin to ridicule him in the presence of the class, make fun of every detail of his presentation, and get the whole class to howl with laughter at the unfortunate Knud, who stood at the blackboard, suffering.

The teacher probably did not know that Knud had much of the Greenlander's nature in him, certainly a lot more than his touch of Eskimo blood would account for. Nothing is worse torture for an Eskimo than to be made the object of ridicule. The entire Eskimo system of litigation is based on making one's opponent the object of laughter. They have big singing competitions in which the object is to sing a laugh-provoking song that will expose the competitors to ridicule. The subject of a wave of laughter suffers deeply. It often happens that the victim of the laughter will move to another place, where his disgrace is not common knowledge.

Knud told me that it was a physical torture for him to go to school on the mornings when he was to have the mathematics class. On one occasion he dawdled so on his way to school that he arrived late and was summoned before the principal to explain his tardiness. A boy does not have the right words to explain something as complicated as that. Knud didn't say a word, and the principal came to the conclusion that Knud had deliberately been late out of a general dislike for school.

He didn't know that the little boy, though happy enough at Mr. Jörgensen's home, had no one to turn to in confidence, but only felt with certainty: "Now I'll be sent in to be tortured, made fun of, and hurt by the teacher's scorn!"

Later in life Knud retained an irrational ill-will toward mathematical formulas. It wasn't that he couldn't master them, but he set up a sort of resistance every time something had to be figured out; and all his life he showed a remarkable tendency to govern his voyages and all his other undertakings by inspiration instead of by dry figuring. He ran the risk and took the consequences, and knew that he could always get out of difficult situations.

The old saying that a diploma alone does not make a great man is best illustrated by Knud Rasmussen. This man who later received doctorates from the Universities of Copenhagen and Edinburgh passed his final examinations with a margin of exactly one point above the lowest passing mark.

By this time, Pastor Rasmussen had been transferred back to Denmark. Knud's little brother Christian was now attending school there. Because Pastor Rasmussen did not receive a very large salary, he called his sons together and explained to them that his economic situation was such that it would be impossible for both of them to continue their studies. He therefore thought that Christian, the younger of the two, should take a preliminary examination and transfer into a technical branch

I SAILED WITH RASMUSSEN

which would not cost so much. But Knud interrupted:

"No, Father," he said, "Christian is more gifted than I, and Christian is much better fitted for a disciplined study career. Let him choose a profession, for I'll be able to take care of myself!"

In this period he struck up a friendship with the two young sons of the famous actor, Emil Poulsen; their names were Adam and Johannes. Through them he developed a strong interest in the theater, and for a while it was his aim and intention to become an actor. He told me about their friendship, which cost him quite a few conscience pangs. The two Poulsen brothers were strict vegetarians, and Knud subscribed to their practice in this regard. But his flesh was weak, and, furthermore, he had been raised on the Greenlandic diet of meat. Therefore, whenever he had a little money—which wasn't very often—he would sneak out of an evening and go to an inexpensive restaurant and order a steak swimming in butter and onions. Potatoes would be served with it, but these he left untouched with grand hauteur and merely enjoyed his meat in mouth-watering bliss, even though later he always felt a certain guilt in not confessing this to his friends.

But Knud did not become an actor. At one point he decided to become a singer. He somehow got the famous singing teacher, Torsleff, to instruct him free of charge. The contract merely stipulated that when Knud became an opera singer, Torsleff would receive one per cent of his income. This, he felt, would be more than enough. So one can see that his expectations were not inconsiderable.

However, things were progressing far too slowly to satisfy Knud's need for action. Therefore, he decided to take a giant leap. Without a penny in his pockets, he went to the Bristol Hotel on City Hall Square and asked to be allowed to take a party up to the second floor music room. He invited Vilhelm Herold, the brilliant opera star, to come and hear him sing. Herold came, and Knud sang.

"This is not exactly a world-shaking baritone," said Herold, "but you do have material that can be developed." And then he left.

This ended Knud's operatic career. But later he apparently felt better about it, for he once told me: "I discovered that I had a much bigger voice than Herold's; he only used his a little better!"

Knud was now an accepted member of aesthetic circles. He had long been a member of Discordia, a discussion club made up of young revolutionaries under the leadership of Marcus Kalckar. The Rindom brothers, Julius Magnussen, the writer Gorki Schmidt, and many others belonged to it.

He also belonged to the Students' Society, where he met a number of men who were later to play a considerable part in Danish cultural life: writers, painters, journalists, and teachers. His appearance, his distinctive facial features, his straightforward thinking (although this sometimes went against the grain of many in these circles) earned him everyone's respect.

He formed a friendship with the writers L. C. Nielsen and Johannes V. Jensen and later remarked:

"I learned so much from those two men, things that I had not known before, that I owe them a great deal."

It was at this time that he made his first trip abroad—a

visit to Berlin. Knud knew very well that a journey to Berlin was expensive and beyond what his father could afford, but he had made up his mind to get to Germany.

Then he remembered that in the garden at the parsonage there was a narwhale skull with two tusks in it. This was a great rarity, for normally only one tooth develops into the famous spiral narwhale horn.

Here, then, was a rare specimen with two tusks. He asked his mother if he could have this skull, and as always the answer was "Yes."

He had figured out that it would be possible for him to get to Berlin for seventy crowns. But he had no idea what this zoological phenomenon could be sold for.

Then he met a school chum on the street, Gregers Winkel, and he asked him if he didn't want to buy a narwhale skull with two tusks. Gregers Winkel, who was a very young man, said right away:

"But since I don't know what a narwhale skull is, it is hard for me to say what I can give you for it. Meet me here in an hour, and I'll be able to tell you what I can pay for it."

An hour later the two friends met again, and Gregers Winkel paid him one hundred crowns. Knud was extremely happy and got to Berlin, where he was further surprised to get another seventy crowns from Gregers Winkel, who had resold the skull for more than he had first anticipated and immediately shared his surplus gains with Knud. Both of these young men were accurately characterized by this transaction. Knud enjoyed the luck that followed him all his life, and Gregers Winkel went on to become a prominent businessman.

Knud told me about this transaction time and again. He valued the experience highly, because in the circles he frequented it was customary to look upon businessmen as profit seekers exclusively.

When he got back he had decided that he wanted to become a writer. Naturally Greenland lay behind this resolve; he had been born there, after all, and not a day passed without his longing for the land. He wanted to travel in his beloved Greenland and to write about his travels.

In 1900 the Students' Society organized a voyage to Iceland, which was much talked about at that time. The century year was to be celebrated, and a closer union between Denmark and Iceland was to be encouraged by the students' visit. Mylius-Erichsen was the leader of the group, but Knud Rasmussen was along as a correspondent for the *Christian Daily,* a post his father had secured for him.

Mylius-Erichsen later told me that Knud caused him quite a bit of difficulty on that trip, because he was always telling everybody glowing tales about Greenland and the many delights to be found there. Now that they were so close, why not have the trip culminate in a visit to Greenland?

For the young man without any responsibility, that was an easy question to ask. Mylius-Erichsen knew very well that Greenland was close to them, but their insurance did not cover a trip there and the funds available covered only the trip to Iceland. He had to take Knud aside and explain these things to him before he would stop agitating for an extension of the trip.

Soon after Knud returned, he left the *Christian Daily* and became a correspondent for the *Illustrated Times*. In this capacity, he was sent to Stockholm to cover the winter sports events held there and known as the Nordic Games. The trip was paid for by the *Illustrated Times,* but he had to use most of his own money to buy pictures to illustrate his articles, and he wrote diligently and interestingly.

He took the initiative in trying to have dog sled driving introduced as an event in the games. But he was put aside with the objection that dog sled driving was neither entertaining nor exciting. He was amused by this assertion, since he knew that those opposed to it had their information from some members of an expedition who had spent a troublesome time behind a team of unruly dogs.

When Knud had been in Stockholm for a short time, he found that he couldn't get along on the funds he had available. He had made friends with a foreign journalist, and the two of them would frequent the smaller restaurants and order the least expensive items—salads or odds and ends from obscure corners of the menu. Since they both looked like foreigners, they were taken to be a pair of refined gourmets who knew how to eat foreign fare properly. But even this could not go on when the money ran out.

He then wrote home to the offices of the *Illustrated Times,* asking them to send him some money and awaited the answer in great suspense, both hungry and anxious. It finally arrived in the form of forty Danish crowns. He had bought pictures on credit for about two hundred crowns, and in addition he had had to live and pay his travel expenses.

41

So pressing was his need and so great were his obligations that these forty crowns meant absolutely nothing. He therefore put them in a large envelope and wrote in large letters:

"FROM SUCH A POVERTY-STRICKEN PUBLICATION I NEITHER CAN NOR WILL ACCEPT ANY PAYMENT."

And he never heard from the *Illustrated Times* again.

That same evening an official banquet was held by the officials of Stockholm for the visiting press. However, only the representatives of the large, famous newspapers were invited, and certainly Knud Rasmussen was not among them. But he wanted to use this opportunity to get a free meal, since the hosts could hardly notice one little mouth more or less.

At the appointed time he appeared at the entrance. The watchful officials at the door stopped him and wanted to see his invitation, but such things never posed any difficulties for Knud.

"I am a foreign journalist," he said with a frown. Then he was told that the others had come dressed in white tie and tails. This saved him; for he now launched into a long harangue about what an unfortunate impression it would make in the foreign press and in his country's chancery if it were made known that a guest, come to report on the Nordic Games, was turned away because he was traveling light. Naturally, a group of very courteous Swedes rushed over and apologized for the conduct of the doorkeepers. There was no further question about an invitation; all efforts were bent toward placating the offended guest.

Knud was seated in a brilliant assemblage and had next to him a fine old gentleman, who turned out to be the head of the Swedish National Railways. Knud's charm, his frank admission that although he had always wanted to go to Lapland he could not afford to make the trip, and his whole unique personality led the amiable rail chief to extend him an invitation to make the trip as a guest of the Swedish National Railways.

During the festivities a number of official speeches were heard and many worthy and weighty words were spoken, but Knud was of the opinion that, if the evening were to become a really festive one, the right things had to be said. Since the speeches were pre-scheduled, he naturally could not get the floor. He was the youngest journalist there, and by far the least prosperous. Notwithstanding, he stole the floor and started his speech. This immediately aroused the resentment of the hosts, but they listened politely, and when he was finished, there wasn't a single person present who was not enthusiastic. Waves of applause flowed over his head. In one evening Knud had become a personage, not only in Stockholm, but in the eyes of journalists from many countries; they vied to make his acquaintance and flocked around him.

At this banquet he met Sweden's great artist and author, Albert Engstrom. They became friends from the outset, and Knud wrote an article about Engstrom for the well-known publication *Strix*. The arrangement was that *Strix* would take care of his hotel bill. Knud Rasmussen was a free man again.

This enabled him to accept the invitation of the Swedish National Railways and make his first trip to Lapland, since he had, in the meantime, entered into an arrangement with *Berlingske Tidende* and received money from them which would finance his stay there. His trip to Lapland became a great adventure and the introduction to the lifework that made him famous.

Up in Lapland he encountered people who reminded him of Eskimos, and their homes soon became his. Their nature was the same, even though details of their way of life differed.

The sale of liquor was prohibited in Lapland. But he soon realized that smugglers rode around at night, rousing people by knocking at their windows, and sold bottles of something they called "dynamite," which was powerful enough to knock the best of them off their feet.

Once Knud was traveling in a railway car along with some of the day laborers who moved from place to place on railway construction jobs. These were people without a fixed abode, people with no idea except "now." Neither "before" nor "after" had any meaning for them. They had to be tremendously strong and tough to compete with each other in the work and also, during their free time, in the fighting and the drinking.

These terrible fellows brought out a couple of bottles and passed them around from mouth to mouth. They were also passed to Knud, who politely said, "No, thank you."

His refusal transformed them from laughing fellow-passengers into raging, violent madmen. To save his skin, Knud had to put the bottle to his lips and take a deep draught, which made him quite drunk and he fell asleep almost immediately. Fortunately he was put off the train at his destination, though without his knowing it.

From Lapland he went over to Narvik, the Norwegian city that exports all the Swedish ore. He traveled there by reindeer. On that trip, he later told me, he missed his Greenland dogs. Reindeer are only a substitute for all other draught animals. They are slow and they are unreliable. Knud Rasmussen drove west with a Lapp friend, but he, too, had learned to drive reindeer.

The reindeer that are used for travel are very large animals. Knud's reindeer had a bad temperament, and during the trip it went mad. It turned around and attacked its passengers. Knud and his friend had to lift up the sled, quick as lightning, throw themselves face down in the snow with the sled over them, and lie still and wait while the reindeer attacked the bottom of the sled with horns and hooves. When the reindeer's wrath had passed, they righted the sled and continued the journey.

From Narvik Knud went up to Tromsö. He remained there quite a while, although circumstances willed it so, for he had not planned to stay. He arrived by steamer, and was to continue on with it, but while waiting he went on a walking tour to see the town. He got lost in the outskirts of the town and didn't know how to get back to the steamer. Then he saw a young girl coming toward him who, he thought, could tell him the way. But she became frightened and crossed to the other side of the street in order to avoid him. He, too, went over to the other side of the street. She turned and fled, and Knud followed close behind. She turned into a little side street and began to run. Knud overtook her very quickly, and grabbed her by the arm. She turned the sweetest face up to him and cried, full of fear:

"Oh, please! Don't do anything to me!"

He then explained to her that he didn't have murder or anything like it in mind and that he only wanted to ask her the way down to the harbor, to the steamer which was to carry him southward.

It was his appearance that had frightened the poor girl. He was dressed in a Lapp skin coat and a pair of stoker's trousers, which he had got in trade on the steamer for his reindeer shoes.

He managed to reassure the girl, and it turned out that she was going down to the harbor, too, so they went on together. When they had been walking for about fifteen minutes, Knud said, "Listen, let's not go down to the steamer. Let's sit down some place and be together for a while."

They went up to Charlottenborg in Tromsö, a meeting place for young people during the skiing season. There they drank tea, and soon a large party had assembled. The steamer left without Knud.

There followed a grand time in Tromsö. Twenty years later he always had with him on his travels in Greenland an old worn-out briefcase with the inscription: "HE-BOM'S HOTEL, TROMSÖ." It was probably stolen from the hotel. How many important papers we both have carried in it, and how often he has talked about it! Once I managed to get it away from him; I had it repaired and gave it back to him on his fiftieth birthday.

When Knud got home from his trip he rented an attic room in Copenhagen where he lived as a bohemian. It was difficult to make ends meet. He worked diligently at writing articles no one would print and stories no one would buy. Then he undertook to write a whole book about his travels in northern Sweden and Norway. He wrote day and night, and as usual he cheated himself of sleep.

There existed at that time a popular periodical called *Health,* which coined and circulated catch phrases such as "Sleep Is Milk!" Knud gave this some thought, and said to one of his friends in his deep voice:

"Maybe that's so, but then maybe milk is also sleep!" From then on he used to buy himself a bottle of skimmed milk, drink it, write, and go without sleep.

When the book was finished he proudly sent it to a publishing company, but it was returned with a letter saying that they would be glad to publish it if he would cover part of the expenses with a deposit of three hundred crowns.

Knud turned to his father who had read the book and asked him to lend him the three hundred crowns.

"Certainly not!" Pastor Rasmussen declared. "This book is far too good for you to have to pay to have it appear. Just let it wait, and you'll see, its time will come."

And its time did come. Years later, when his book *New Peoples* had become a great success and was looked upon as a classic, Knud's first opus was bought for a large sum.

~~~~~~

When Knud was twenty-three years old, he was invited by his old friend Mylius-Erichsen, who had led the students' tour to Iceland and was now a journalist on the staff of the *Politiken,* to go along on an expedition to West Greenland.

This journey was to be called "The Literary Expedition to West Greenland," chiefly because Mylius-Erichsen's purpose was to write a series of articles about conditions there and life among the Eskimos.

Organizing a journalistic expedition was extremely difficult because since the beginning of the Danish colonization of Greenland by the missionary Hans Egede, in 1721, Greenland had been a closed land. Denmark had aimed to aid Greenland in cultural respects so as to enable its inhabitants gradually to establish contact with the outside world without becoming subject to exploitation. For this reason, the only outsiders allowed into Greenland were Danish officials and missionaries. No journalists had ever gone there, and many well-meaning people thought that it was best for the country and for its inhabitants if they were left alone and had as little contact as possible with civilization.

The Director of Greenlandic Affairs did what he could to prevent the voyage from taking place. But new ideas had taken hold in Denmark, and the expedition set out. It included Dr. Alfred Bertelsen and the painter, Count Harald Moltke. The latter, who had already been to South Greenland, Lapland, and Iceland, became Knud's lifelong friend. Knud was the youngest of the four men.

When they reached Knud's birthplace, Jakobshavn, they set up headquarters and got hold of some dog teams and proceeded to the district around Disko Bay. Knud had the advantage over the others in that he spoke the language as a native, knew how to drive dog teams, and knew the entire population personally.

In Godthaab, several hundred miles south of God-havn, Mylius-Erichsen had taken on Knud's childhood friend, the Greenlander Jörgen Brönlund, as an interpreter. His Danish was not entirely faultless, but he had an advantage over other Greenlandic interpreters in that he translated fearlessly and unhesitatingly whatever was said. Greenlanders have a weakness in that they cannot bear to say anything unpleasant to anybody. Even when they are acting as interpreters they tend to edit an unpleasant statement and tone down sharp utterances. Knud hated to serve as an interpreter. He had always hated it, and he always continued to hate it. Jörgen Brönlund therefore took over this work.

Mylius-Erichsen was a remarkable man, and often he would get very strange ideas which had to be carried out at once. He wanted to take a trip across Disko Island. They started out from Godhavn. Mylius-Erichsen was a poor dog driver, and on the way Jörgen Brönlund became restive, which is something that often happened. They ran into bad weather and had to pitch camp in the mountains. The tent blew down. Some of the dogs gnawed their way to freedom, chewing into bits the harness, reins, and whips. Mylius raged, and everything got worse. The days passed and provisions ran out. They ate the dog fodder, and then they had to slaughter the rest of the dogs. The entire distance was no greater than ordinarily can be covered in one day.

When they reached Qeqertak, Uncle Carl and Aunt Augustine supplied their favorite nephew with the finest fur clothing and the softest moccasins; but Knud was not one to be satisfied with receiving things himself; he got the whole expedition outfitted out of his good aunt's limitless stores. Uncle Carl gave Knud twelve beautiful dogs, snow white and with big heads, all of the same size and faster than any other dogs on the whole west coast. Carl considered Knud's prowess with dogs his greatest personal triumph.

From Qeqertak they drove up over Majoren, which is the mountain pass leading to the famous Umanak Fjord. The first place they reached was Ikerasak, where Knud Rasmussen's other uncle, the renowned Jens Fleischer, lived.

If Uncle Carl had been good, then Uncle Jens was better. Uncle Carl had given them much, because he was well-to-do; Uncle Jens gave too, but he was poor. He was a lover of life and rich in friends, and he was the best dog driver in North Greenland. He thought he saw himself reborn in his nephew Knud. As an active young man he had accompanied the world-famous alpine climber Whymper across the central ice. Of this trip he remembered only that he got terrible food and excellent wine; they didn't get very far, because Whymper got cold.

There was a comradeship between him and Knud as though they were the same age. The differences between their means, their culture, and their way of life were blotted out by a deep affection. Knud always helped himself to anything of Uncle Jens's; in return, he often settled pressing debts for his uncle, who hardly thanked him—it was so natural that it should be thus—but continued to live and to enjoy life.

Then they were to cross the Svartenhuk Peninsula to Upernavik.

Whenever the expedition arrived at a settlement, big or small, the inhabitants came rushing out and greeted Knud with loud cries, quite forgetting that there were others in the party. They gave him dog fodder and seals for his dogs only. It was true that he was a much better driver than the others, but he divided what he got with the others, ignoring the natives' reward for his prowess as a handler of dogs.

On the way Mylius-Erichsen wrote; Dr. Bertelsen examined the people they encountered, who seldom or never were visited by doctors; Moltke painted; and Jörgen Brönlund interpreted. Only Knud did nothing definite or systematic. He was so unspeakably happy just to be there that he reveled in the Greenlandic speech and way of life and took most of his meals with the Eskimos.

51

They arrived at Upernavik, where Governor Kraul received them. Here they settled down for a while. The expedition was divided up. Dr. Bertelsen went south to continue his medical research, the others wanted to go out into the unknown, up to the strange Eskimos about whom legends circulated in the Danish part of Greenland. These were the heathen people that the old women with quaking voices had told Knud about when he was a child, the people he had resolved, at the age of ten, to visit as soon as his dogs were grown!

But for the time being Upernavik was their headquarters. Knud turned the whole colony upside down. A series of parties and celebrations, the likes of which had never been seen, were arranged, culminating in a carnival, in which everyone was obliged to appear in three different costumes during the course of the evening. Only the pastor and his wife were excused.

The festivities over, the expedition drove northward. They stopped at Kûk, where Simon Bearhunter had his house. Simon was the northernmost inhabitant in colonized Greenland, and if anyone moved to a place north of him, he would move still farther north. He brought in more bear skins than anyone else. He was always a pleasant host, and a dignified man.

Mylius-Erichsen wanted an extra sled to come along to carry the necessary baggage, and Simon ordered his nephew Gaba to go along.

So at last Knud was doing what he had dreamed of since his childhood days—making a long sled journey with good dogs up to the land of the heathen Eskimos.

Mylius-Erichsen was not a notable cartographer or navigator, and nobody at that time knew anything about prevailing conditions. But they went ahead through unknown territory and endured the hardships of the journey: the difficult terrain, the dogs eating their harnesses at night, the men freezing in tents because they didn't know enough to build themselves warm snow houses. In short, they experienced all the difficulties arising out of inexperience. They were impractically outfitted.

Both Knud and Jörgen Brönlund were excellent dog trainers, and had trained their dogs in bear signals all during the journey. A bear signal is a sound emitted by the driver when there is evidence of game in the vicinity. Drivers train the dogs by repeating the signal over and over while the going is light, and the dogs then take to galloping. Once the dogs have followed bear tracks and have tasted the bear's delicious, warm flesh immediately after the bear has been shot, they will forever after show a great eagerness to relive this experience.

They brought in several polar bears around Melville Bay, one of the world's best bear-hunting districts. The west wind pushes the ice across from Lancaster Sound or Jones Sound, and every fall large numbers of bears come across, driven by their restless natures.

But now the expedition began to be plagued by misfortune; the dog teams fell prey to disease. Even worse, Harald Moltke became sick. But with his tremendous energy, he refused to give up. Mylius-Erichsen needed sketches of the scenery for his publications, and Moltke produced them as long as he was able. In his youthful self-confidence, he thought of himself as unconquerable, and very often he sat for hours at a time out on the freezing cliffs or on the top of ice mountains, sketching until he became chilled through and through.

Finally, he was unable to eat in the evening or to sleep at night. The others lay freezing in the sleeping-bags, but Moltke lay burning with fever, and at last he began to rave.

It was Knud's energy and will that pushed them on to human habitation in time to save Moltke. It must be deemed a miracle that Moltke was kept alive.

Among the polar Eskimos Knud made friends with a whole new people. He embraced the whole country in his youthful exuberance. The expedition built a headquarters building on Saunders Island; the ruins are still standing. It was a poor house to look at, but it was cozy and pleasant inside.

Knud was something of an experience for the Eskimos to encounter. He was the best dog driver they had ever seen, and in reindeer hunts he impressed them all with his marksmanship. They considered him to be the natural leader of the expedition, because the Eskimos always think most highly of those who are proficient at their own skills and know how to use the weapons that bring them their livelihood.

The journey back from the north was a terribly bad one. It was dark, and there was very little feed for the dogs. This was the first time that Knud had a party of Eskimos with him and had to make decisions for them. In spite of darkness and weather the party succeeded in reaching Tasiussaq.

The things that Knud lived through on the expedition became constant factors throughout his later life. He came to love the heathen people and all that pertained to them, and in the next few years he made several trips north to learn more about them.

When Knud got back to Denmark after the Literary Expedition, he was the most sought-after young man in Copenhagen, and he had many, many friends.

They all used to go out to Knud's father's parsonage at Lynge, outside of Copenhagen. It is a fact that a young man's choice of friends rarely matches his parents' choice; it often happened that the good parson and his wife found their son's comrades somewhat different from what they might have wished, but they never criticized.

"Bring them home," they said to their children, "bring your friends with you, because we know that those you ask to your home are people you value for some reason or other. We know there must be something worth knowing in all of them, even though it is often difficult for us to recognize what it is!"

They were wise parents, and life proved them right. Among the young people who visited, the children of the pastor at the nearby town of Birkeröd were among the dearest. Knud was a friend of Herluf, who was of the same age; May got engaged to Herluf's younger brother, Jens, and Christian to Herluf's sister, Rachel.

A lot of other young folks came out to Lynge.

One of them, a young lady, made a great impression on Knud. Her name was Dagmar Andersen, and she was the daughter of an important man—the State Counselor at Söholm, Chairman of the Employers' Association, and one of Denmark's major entrepreneurs. But Dagmar Andersen was very modest and unassuming. She never sought to make her presence or her family's importance felt. In the gay crowd that surrounded Knud, she functioned as a breath of common sense without ever being cool or sitting in judgment on them; she was a wonderful human being.

Knud and Dagmar were married in the fall of 1908. And this marriage was for him a source of strength of which perhaps no other person can realize the value or understand. Dagmar, his faithful wife, whose lot it so often was to sit anxiously at home while her husband was away for years at a time, was his comrade and friend. She was certainly the only person in the world who could fill the place at his side both at home and before the world, during the time when they had only modest means as well as later, when all the lands of the world vied in honoring and inviting him. She was fine and good and faithful from that first day until his eyes were closed in death.

4

~~~~~~

It was the year after his marriage that I met Knud. He was then thirty years old.

In the winter of 1910, he made a proposal to me that, as I have said before, changed the entire course of my life. His idea was to go up to the west coast of Greenland, north of Melville Bay, appropriate land for Denmark and live in the northernmost inhabited area of the world. At that time, Denmark was in possession of the only colonized area of Greenland on the west coast south of Melville Bay. Any foreign nation that pleased could have taken possession of the rest of Greenland, though no nation could have afforded to maintain officials for such few natives as existed outside the Danish colony.

He thought he had a way for us to support ourselves up there and asked me to become his partner in an undertaking to establish a trading station among the Polar Eskimos in the extreme north of Greenland. It was his idea to exchange our modern tools, equipment and weapons, to which Admiral Peary had introduced the natives, in return for their furs. Knud's main purpose, however, was not commercial but scientific. He had decided to make the study of the Eskimo—not only in Greenland but on the entire North American continent—his life's work.

I thought about it for several days. I had myself to think of and my future. I realized that I had an opportunity to make a living in the civilized world. I could complete my studies at the university. Or I could become a sailor. I might even make a name for myself as a newspaperman. I might do any number of things.

But I decided against all these possibilities. The spirit of adventure was my heritage. My grandfather, something of a wanderer himself, had inspired in me a desire to seek out the strange and the different.

I told Knud I would go with him—and I never regretted my decision.

There was one big obstacle, however—the lack of financial backing. We tried to get a government grant, but had no success.

We were in a hurry because a Norwegian explorer, the famous Otto Sverdrup, was planning a similar undertaking. We had heard of his intention to establish a sealing station on Saunders Island in Northwestern Greenland where he could make most profitable deals with "our" Eskimos. And Knud was afraid that Sverdrup's activities would give Norway a foothold in Greenland, making it harder to bring the whole island of Greenland under Danish rule.

Knud's fears actually materialized, though many years

later and not due to Sverdrup. In 1931 a group of Norwegian hunters, on their own initiative, occupied a section
of the northeastern coast of Greenland in the name of the
Norwegian king, and after some hesitation the Norwegian
government recognized the occupation. Denmark at once
summoned Norway into the International Court of Justice
at The Hague, and in 1933 the Norwegian occupation was
found invalid and Danish sovereignty was recognized as
extending over both the colonized and uncolonized areas
of Greenland.

Knud and I carefully figured out the minimum amount
we needed and thought we had found a way to get it.

With optimism as our only asset, we set out on a lecture
tour. The discovery of the North Pole in 1909 had aroused
a thirst for knowledge of the Arctic.

I engaged lecture halls throughout Denmark and had
posters and programs printed—on credit. We carried slides
and a projector that did not work properly. It showed only
a few black spots on the screen. But Knud was, as usual,
master of the situation and announced calmly to the audience that we were the first men to show slides from Greenland as it really is in the winter when there is no light
for months!

"Yes, ladies and gentlemen," said Knud, "I'm sure you
have seen many beautiful pictures from the Arctic regions,
but this evening we shall show you some realistic pictures
from the period of darkness, when all contours merge, so
that one hardly knows what is to be found quite nearby."

I showed some dancing Eskimo women in the summertime. The audience was informed by Knud that this was
a hunter at a seal's breathing hole in the darkness of

winter. I succeeded in making some light and shadow visible. This was a dog driver under way.

An old provincial actor had told us that to insure success a tour must begin either in Odder or Slagelse. We followed his advice, but only three towns got the benefit of our projector, and then we had to engage a projectionist who accompanied us during the rest of the tour. We covered all of Denmark, and in every town there would be a celebration, and everywhere Knud collected admirers.

It was a wonderful tour, after which we had little more cash than when we set out. The situation was saved, finally, by two goods friends—a lady in Copenhagen, who gave us half the sum we needed, and an engineer by the name of Nyboe who supplied the balance.

We found a small ship with a crew of six which was cheap enough to charter but otherwise totally unsuited for any excursion to the Arctic. The rudder was made of thin metal plates which were unable to withstand any ice pressure. We completed the purchases of our equipment and supplies and the minimum of goods needed to open a trading station. Our capital was soon nearly exhausted and we had to keep a small reserve for emergencies. When we were ready to leave, our supplies were pitifully small, but we had optimism and youth, not to mention the faith of our friends.

And thus, in the summer of 1910, we sailed for the Arctic.

We were thrilled to be on our way, even though a heavy debt to our generous benefactors rested on our shoulders. We were young and still believed that life would reward us with a reality equal to our dreams. One day we found ourselves close enough to the southern coast of Greenland to view Cape Farewell. That point is seldom seen, for ships ordinarily keep far away from the coast in order to avoid the ice. Even when the immediate water is clear, the polar ice lies to the south as far as the eye can see; the prevailing wind is from the southwest, and it may blow the pack in before a ship has an opportunity to get clear. We saw the huge mountains on shore, an ominous foreboding of the sternness of the land. The sea ran high and the rocks offered no solace. They are black and towering, and there is no pity in them. As I stood at the wheel I realized for the first time that I had burned my bridges and was up against something which would demand the utmost from me.

We ran into the ice and out again. We all worked desperately; the crew understood that a wreck would benefit them no more than it would us.

We landed first at Godhavn where I bought some dogs and a few supplies we had neglected to purchase at home. Knud refused even to look at the dogs, for he planned to stop at Qeqertak and get far superior dogs from his Uncle Carl.

In Godhavn we were approached by a woman named Vivi who was the daughter of Hans Henrik, famous in his time for having taken part in eight American expeditions to the north, and an Eskimo woman; Vivi had married into a Cape York tribe, but was now a widow. She asked to be taken along.

"We don't dare take you along," said Knud, "because we don't know what kind of conditions we will be living under."

"Oh," said Vivi, "I am alone in the world and have no husband to hunt for me, so things could not be worse than they are now."

"You are the right one for us," said Knud, and we took along Vivi and her eleven-year-old son. Vivi was to be our housekeeper when we got ourselves settled.

Next we stopped to visit Knud's Uncle Carl in Qeqertak. We secured dogs and dog food and clothes from him.

What a time we spent there! The games and dancing lasted for days. Uncle Carl was famous for his skill as a marksman, and he always asked his guests to hang their pipes for targets on nails atop the fence posts around the dog yard. He was never happier than when he had to furnish his friends new pipes because he had shot their old ones to bits. Uncle Carl also had a two-piece orchestra— himself on a violin and his daughter on an accordion. They played for us all through the night.

Qeqertak is situated in a fjord dotted with floating icebergs, and our captain was no particular admirer of the anchorage. Yet we dared not depart before the hospitality was at an end—Uncle Carl felt that any criticism of the fjord was a direct reflection on himself. As a result, we stayed longer than we should have.

From Qeqertak we sailed off into parts unknown.

In order to penetrate farther north the voyager must traverse Melville Bay which is a stretch of water considered by whalers to be the most dangerous in the Arctic. Ice blocks crowd the water the year round, and we feared for our ship, which was certainly no ice jammer. But we continued to forge ahead, since so long as one remains on the Greenland side of the bay the current puts him to the north. It is a well-known fact that in Arctic waters the current follows him who keeps land to starboard.

We got across Melville Bay without mishap, but then we ran into a fierce gale that whipped our sails, and our weak motor was no match for it. Where we were driven I have never discovered, and it is a miracle that we were not thrown up onto the Parry Islands or that we got through at all. In the middle of the storm our boat was tossed against an iceberg and our rudder cracked. I ran out to try to take in the foresails, but at that moment chunks of ice broke from the berg and, churning about in the water, cracked off our propeller blades like the daintiest chips.

And there we were, powerless in the gale. Suddenly the wind increased, as it often does in the far north, and blew us straight into a snug little harbor, North Star Bay, which served the Eskimo settlement of Thule.

We were seen by the natives and they ran out to greet us. They had spotted us the day before tossing about in the storm but thought we had surely been wrecked by now, and they had tried to figure out where they might find some of the wreckage and lumber that would drift in. "If we had known Knud Rasmussen was on board," they said, "we would have realized he would make harbor."

We unloaded our goods and settled down. We had not planned to make Thule our station, but we had no alternative; afterward we found it to be the best location in the whole district. It was possible to bank the boat at low tide and screw two new blades onto the propeller, and after a few days we watched it sail away leaving us, two lone white men, in a little world of North Greenland Eskimos.

Top: An iceberg in the Thule district.
Bottom: The seacoast at Thule.

We built a house on shore; it was not very big nor very comfortable, so we spent as little time in it as possible. Still, during the long winter months it was warm enough inside.

The district we were to serve with our trading post reached as far north as any natives lived, and as far south as Melville Bay. At the time of our arrival only a scant two hundred persons inhabited this territory and were scattered far from one another up and down the coast. Only four families lived at our settlement.

The Eskimos were already more advanced in many ways than I had expected. I remember, for example, that we had a globe along, a gift from Mr. Nyboe. It was standing on a box outside the tents we set up while we were building our houses, and one day I noticed that a group of people had collected around it and that an old man was pointing to the South Pole. Then, wise young man that I was, I went over to them and began, in my poor Eskimo-ese, to explain that the globe represented the earth and that they were up here, and so on; but I was stopped by Knud, who came up to me and said that I didn't have to tell them anything, because the old man was giving them a lecture about conditions at the South Pole. Somewhat shamed I withdrew.

I learned quickly to live in Eskimo fashion. The first day we were there Knud beamingly informed me that an Eskimo named Samik had gone to fetch some rotten meat which was two years old—a feast to mark our coming.

I closed my eyes and my heart jumped up to my throat when I began to eat. When I stopped eating my eyes were still closed, because I had eaten so much that I could not keep them open.

One of our first problems was to secure meat for our dogs. That is, in fact, the greatest problem in the North. Eskimos take great pride in their dogs and keep far too many of them. Humans and dogs eat exactly the same things, but the amount consumed by the natives is trifling compared with what the dogs require.

Our dogs still had full sets of teeth, and we were asked by the natives to cut them off or dull them. In the south of Greenland the dogs run wild the whole summer—and winter too, when not in use—and forage for themselves, eating anything except wood, stone and iron. But where we lived the rules were different. Here the dogs were tied up so that things could be left about without the dogs consuming them.

It is impossible to tie dogs with sealskin lines if the animals have the full use of their teeth. Therefore the long sharp teeth which a dog uses for tearing and slashing must be dulled. This is accomplished easily with puppies by using a stone or a file to flatten them. But ours were full-grown dogs, and the operation had to be performed with a hammer. To handle the poor animal for this operation, he must be stupefied—hung by the neck until he is unconscious. This state is reached when his excrement drops from him. Then he is hurriedly let down, his jaws pried apart and held by two skin lines, while his teeth are flattened with a hammer. This is, of course, a cruel operation, but it apparently does not result in any serious after-effects. Time after time I have seen them jump up when they regain consciousness and run off to eat or fight or whatever comes into their minds.

Because their teeth have been dulled, the dogs cannot eat frozen meat in winter, and it is always a matter of great concern to thaw it for them. They are fed mostly on walrus hide cut into chunks. They are fed in a group so that, in order to get enough, each animal must wolf his food without waiting to masticate it. While to the casual observer this seems unnecessarily cruel, the scheme is entirely practical. Since the animals are unable to chew, the meat requires a long time for digestion and remains in their stomachs for several days; thus the dogs do not feel hungry as frequently as they would if they chewed the meat.

On sledge trips we fed our dogs every second day, and at home, during the winter when they were doing no work, every third day. In summer, when they were tethered along a brook or at some pond, they needed to be fed no oftener than once a week. They were never as good on trips after they had been fed as when they were hungry.

Remember that the Thule District—as it was named because it is the northernmost in the world—is not teeming with game. Sometimes days pass with nothing to eat, and if dogs are accustomed to food only every other day they can go without for four days and feel no worse than we do when we miss a single meal.

We spent the fall of 1910 collecting meat. Because the big killings are made in the spring, we had to depend largely upon the natives for our supply. We soon learned that the simplest method of bragging about his hunting exploits is for an Eskimo to stuff his visitors' dogs so full of meat that they can eat no more. And so we took our dogs visiting very frequently that fall.

It was always delightful, too, when the Eskimos visited us. Knud had made many friends on his previous expeditions with whom we did not stand on ceremony; we were at their houses regularly and they came streaming in to us all the time.

A friend, Agparlerssuarssuk, soon arrived with his family. "We are moving in," he said, "because I used up my provisions. I know that you don't have very much, but at any rate you have more than I, and besides, I prefer your house to mine!" And so he remained over the winter.

After our house was put in livable shape, we left Vivi in charge and set out separately into the surrounding country to let the natives know we were there and to procure additional meat for the winter. We also were prepared to make scientific investigations and collect specimens of various sorts for the museums at home.

We decided that I should try to cross Melville Bay by dog sled that winter and secure from the government post at Tasiussaq a number of supplies we had neglected to bring with us from Denmark. The time of year was favorable because, in spite of the darkness, we had a bright moon and calm skies. Knud was to remain at the post during my absence.

When I returned to Thule several weeks later Knud's welcome was heart-warming. He should have been an organizer of parties. In fact, he was the Arctic Elsa Maxwell, for he was never happier than when he could celebrate something or other, and I never knew a man who could find so many occasions for celebration. All the natives were summoned and our stories and laughter rang out until morning.

Yet in the group there was one face I missed—that of a certain young girl. I inquired about her, the stepdaughter of Uvdluriark, our helper at the trading post.

But next day I met her as she walked on the ice with her little brother slung on her back. When she saw me she hid behind an ice ridge. I started round to find her but she ran as fast as she could go. She was hampered by the child on her back, and it was easy for me to catch her and hold her.

"Why did you run away?" I demanded.

"I don't know."

"Are you afraid of me? You need not be!"

"No, I am not afraid, but someone told that you had inquired for me yesterday before everyone. Therefore I was embarrassed!"

"I must know your name—what is it?"

"Oh, I am nobody, just the most ugly and foolish girl in the tribe."

"I don't think so, but what is your name?"

"I don't know."

"You mean you don't know your own name?"

"No, I never heard it."

"Nonsense," I persisted. "Of course you know your name. Why won't you tell it to me?"

"Others can tell it to you, but it is not important."

"I brought something back for you, something you will like."

"Oh, no, don't give me anything," she begged. "Give it to somebody worth giving things!"

And while I searched in desperation for a means of

breaking through her self-abnegation, she made a quick movement and disappeared in the dark.

Later on I asked one of the girls at our house about her name. She, too, refused to tell me, explaining politely, "You are making yourself ridiculous asking for a young woman's name."

I later found out that her name was Mequpaluk.

We lived contentedly in our little house, and never shall I be so happy again. Perhaps most men could not have endured the isolation, but I had everything I wanted—friendship, trust and a busy, active life. We did not cheat the Eskimos, for they were our friends, and they came to us for the fulfillment of their wants.

By now, we had in our household three women—Vivi, Arnajark, an elderly woman who had been Knud's servant on one of his earlier trips to Greenland, and Aloqisaq, who had recently lost her husband.

Arnajark was put in charge of the natives—or rather, she put herself in that position. Vivi did the cooking, and a fine cook she was too. Arnajark chose the place closest to the window so that she could be the one "who calls out when a visitor arrives, and tells who it is."

Everyone in the village visited us daily. When a man did not come, we could be sure he was out hunting. Strangers came from great distances to trade goods and stories. Our stock of trading material was limited as we had little money to fit out our post, but everyone was happy to see us whether we had anything or not. "Now we are like the southerners and have a store nearby," the natives would say. Some even questioned our prices, and

Knud and Arnajark outside our house at Thule.

others insisted upon paying more than we asked so that they could boast of the value of their belongings.

Of course, there were a few who had visited far to the south and seen real stores beyond Tasiussaq. They said that if we were real traders we should have a scale to weigh our goods. Didn't genuine stores always weigh everything?

Knud, never at a loss, could answer this criticism: "You see, all our goods have been weighed before they were packed."

We saw our supply of goods diminishing, and Arnajark warned us: "Don't sell too much. It will never do for some people to have more than we do. How may we take any pleasure from life if we trade our precious things for nothing but foxes, which run loose in the mountains winter and summer?" That was certainly, from her point of view, good logic.

5

Later that winter, when Knud was to leave for Ellesmere Land to hunt musk oxen, I decided to accompany
him part of the way. We sent out word to the north
and south that we would both be gone for a while and set
out by dog sledge with Uvdluriark.

The ice was solid and we made Cape Parry the first day.
The first night we slept in a cave, and next day reached
Natsilivik, a famous Arctic community around which
countless legends and traditions have grown up. No other
place has so many murders to its discredit, and upon the
big stones outside the houses may be seen the footprints of
the famous conjurer, the angakok, who is believed to have
come here to escape from the devil, Tornarsuk. He had
such power and strength that his feet made a deep impression in the stones for the skeptics to view.

At Natsilivik lived old man Sorqaq whose fame had
reached me before I came to Greenland. He had once been

the greatest hunter and angakok in the tribe, and had never ceased to resent the invasion of natives from Admiralty Bay who had brought with them the kayak and the bow and arrow, and had colored the lives of the people who had been here before them. Sorqaq never adopted the new ways, and consequently the newcomers had usurped a great deal of his glory. He was still, however, the best dog breeder of the tribe, and boasted a team of black dogs superior to any man's. This had eased his passage into old age, and he did not complain.

When we arrived at Natsilivik he was ailing. He had been out on a long hunting trip with a number of younger men to the far north—Lady Franklin Bay. Sorqaq, as always, had been far ahead of his companions, and they, suddenly surprised to see him driving back toward them, questioned him. He admitted that he had come to an iceberg and driven his dogs around it, but had forgotten to straighten them out when he reached the other side, and they had completely circled it and backtracked on their course. This had been a crushing blow to Sorqaq, who remarked:

"Such things are foolish. I never was foolish before. I must be growing old!"

He had decided to return home, because he had in his time seen many old men make fools of themselves, and he did not wish his own sons to laugh at him. When he was well enough to go hunting again, he determined always to go alone.

My reputation as a medical student had apparently followed me to Natsilivik, for while there I was asked to go to Ulugassat (Northumberland Island) to take a look at a woman named Alakrasina. She was the widow of an Eskimo called Uvisakavsik who had been murdered by Sigdloo, the Eskimo who had been "number three man" with Peary. After the murder, Sigdloo had taken Alakrasina as his own wife. She was an ill-tempered, hysterical female, and now, it seemed, her right arm was paralyzed. What could I do for this?

She had been Uvisakavsik's favorite wife until he grew tired of her. While she had lived with Uvisakavsik she had become pregnant, but foolishly denied it to the other women. Even long after they could see her condition she refused to admit it, and bragged that Uvisakavsik was such an excellent provider that she was merely growing fatter.

When her time came she had given birth to a boy, but to give truth to her lie she had strangled the child.

I recommended massage for her arm, but at this she scoffed. While she had learned to sew with her left hand, she was such an unpleasant woman that Sigdloo had tried to get rid of her and given her away to other men. They always sent her back, and finally in order to avoid her, her poor husband spent most of his time with his neighbors. His beautiful hair and pleasant manners made him popular with the ladies, while his prowess as a hunter and his reputation as a companion of Peary made him a favorite with the men.

Sigdloo asked Knud for his advice. Should he shoot the brother of Uvisakasvik in order to forestall his revenge?

Knud would not have been the man he was if he had not long ago foreseen this. He had already talked with Samik, the brother of the murdered man, and explained to him that there were to be no murders for revenge. If Samik

Alakrasina.

killed a man, would not he then be murdered? And if
someone killed him, what would become of his little boy?
The child would be fatherless.

Knud persuaded all concerned that it would be best to
do no more killing.

At Natsilivik a small Eskimo whose name was Ukuyak
asked if he could accompany us the rest of the way north.
His wife, Atitak, was pregnant and he was in a hurry to
reach his settlement in time for the birth of his child.
Women in the Arctic never know when their children are
due, but there were unmistakable indications that Ukuyak's wife did not have long to wait. Despite his youth and
smallness, Ukuyak had been with Peary and was famous
as a hunter.

We set off for Nekri, our final destination, Ukuyak and
his wife as well as several other travelers in our party. We
were now in the northern reaches of Polar Eskimo land,
which is divided into three sections defined by their rela-
tion to the southwest wind that prevails over the whole of
Greenland. The Eskimos who live at Cape York and in
Melville Bay are called Nigerdleet—Those Who Live on
the Windy Side. Immediately north are the Akuarmiut—
Those Who Live in Between. This section includes the
land where our post at Thule was situated. And north of
Cape Parry live the Oqonermiut—Those Who Live on the
Leeside.

Those terms are definite and characteristic, but there
are many severe gales on the leeside. Without warning
one intercepted us on the way to Nekri. There were no
clouds in the sky, but suddenly far out to sea the snow
was whisked into the air, and before we had time to make

any preparations the storm was upon us, the atmosphere an unbreathable mixture of snow and blinding ice. My dogs were whipped off their feet and, in spite of my frantic efforts, gathered about the leeside of my sledge. My companions were blotted out by the storm, and I crouched there quite alone, wondering what to do. At last I crawled —it was impossible to stand—ahead and came upon the rest of the party. They were all gathered together holding a conference. When I was near enough to make them hear I yelled as loud as I could to ask their advice.

They had no time for my troubles. Atitak was in labor.

We tried to build an igloo for her, but the snow was so thin that as soon as blocks were cut they were blown to pieces. Somehow I got a glimpse of poor Atitak's face, and I saw on it all the pain and distress a woman feels under such circumstances. She seemed to expect me and Knud to do something for her. And yet what could we do? There was no hope of building a shelter, and it was out of the question for her to undress.

It was a desperate moment and we had to employ desperate measures. We placed Atitak on the leeside of the sledge, and a number of the men grouped themselves upon it to break the wind. We split the woman's pants only as much as was necessary. The bag of water had already broken, and I knew that the moment had come.

Eskimo women always stand on their knees when giving birth, their husbands supporting them from the back and helping to expel the baby. This was Ukuyak's first child and he had no experience, so one of the others, who had several children to his credit, took over the task and pressed the baby out in no time at all. Atitak snatched up

Top: Resting the dogs.
Bottom: Dogdriving.

the child inside her coat, wrapped some skins about him—
it was a man child—and soon had him warm and snug. The
storm abated somewhat, we emptied the load from Knud's
sledge and bade him drive Atitak to Nekri at once to get
her inside a shelter. When we finally reached the village
we found her well and gay, and the boy already slung in
her hood.

Knud left me at Nekri while he went further north for
musk oxen. It was almost spring when he returned, loaded
with skins and enough musk-ox meat for the whole tribe.
His cries and his laughter preceded him and resounded
over the whole place. We all felt that we were better off
when he was with us. His was a tangible force to which we
might cling in the wilderness. We played games in his
honor, and he was always foremost in every kind of sport.
Unfortunately we had a near accident.

A boy walked far out on the ice and hid behind a hum-
mock. Then he jumped up holding a bearskin over his
head with which to tease the dogs.

Such excitement I have seldom seen. Here was an opportunity to prove to the womenfolk who had the best dogs.
The animals were hurriedly hitched to the sledges—probably thirty teams in all—and we were off, shouting and
laughing and lashing the dogs. My team got tangled up
with two others.

The boy should have kept the bearskin over him until
the first team was almost upon him, then discarded it and
saved himself. But he wanted to give an especially fine
performance, and ran about with the pelt still over his
head, dogs hanging onto it ferociously. Many of them bit

through it, and the blood streamed from him. I finally got him free and drove him home while the others remained and watched the dogfights that resulted. Eventually the boy's wounds healed.

Among his many other activities, Knud was writing a book about the traditions, myths, and folklore of the Eskimos. On the way back to Thule he wanted to talk with a certain old woman, Semigak, who was wise in the ways of her people and a great gossip besides. One night, during a raging snowstorm, we stopped at a settlement and were received with enthusiam, as always. After a while, Knud asked our host about Semigak.

"Oh, that poor old woman," he said. "You see, she has very few relatives here and she is alone most of the time. She went out to look after her fox traps before the storm started and she hasn't come home since; her traps are a long way from here. Everybody is sorry for her and now we think that it is better to commiserate with her once and for all and then never feel sorry for her any more."

Knud called me, and we drove out to look for her. The snow had begun to drift and our dogs were difficult to manage, so after a while we decided to seek shelter in a cave along the cliffs where Semigak was known to keep her traps. We drove the dogs up over the ice foot and into the cave, and there we found the poor old woman.

"So, you are here," she said, showing no surprise. All her life she had been a great angakok, and here in the cave she had heard many voices and talked with the spirits of people long dead. This is how she knew we were coming. She had gleaned much information about the living which would enable her to shame them.

81

She had not been especially comfortable, but she was at least still alive. She had trapped and eaten three foxes which she was very sorry had already been dead in the traps when she found them, since she had torn the pelts in skinning them. She had wanted them for her grandson. She had no sleeping bag, but was thankful for her sledge; she could sleep on that. Her strength was exhausted, but her appetite was enormous, and the casual observer might have thought she had only been out for a walk and gotten a little chilly.

We took her along back to the settlement, where Knud ordered all the women to sew her a new dress. She was overwhelmed with the new clothing, and said that she could never remember having looked so well.

Meanwhile our dogs had become sick, and in order to cure them she arranged a séance and so learned that the dogs were sick because they were harnessed in reins that had not been made for them.

It was a fact that we had bought ready-made harnesses. Semigak also announced that our dogs would spread the infection; and so she drafted the entire male population of the settlement to sew new harnesses for us, and we got these free of charge; oddly enough, the dogs got well.

Then the old woman told us that she had made up her mind to go with us.

"You who are new to this land need an experienced woman's protection!"

Next day we started for home. She climbed on Knud's sledge and refused to get off, sitting upon and smashing his camera. When he seemed perturbed over this she immediately took the offensive and scolded him for fooling around with things which could not bear the weight of an old and half-starved woman.

She lived with us for many years. During the darkest days of the winter months she would collect all the boxes and bags she could get hold of.

"I collect shadows and darkness," she said, "so that the world will get light again, and I keep it all locked up here in these boxes." And every spring the sun came back.

A source of strife cropped up at first. She was so full of lice that Knud insisted upon cleaning her up. Her hair had not been combed since the birth of her youngest daughter, who was now married and had her own children, and hence it had to be cut off close to the scalp. I did not witness this operation, but Knud told me that her head "resembled an ant-hill."

Then she was washed several days in a row, and she walked around with a shawl around her head, proud as a little boy with a machine haircut.

Many sledges followed us to Thule. Many natives were already there, waiting to trade with us. One of them came to us and complained: "Your stuff is too cheap! When we had to wait for many years for the whaling ships, and when we had to give all the foxskins we owned for a knife, we were more pleased by the possession of the knife. Now every boy can own a knife, and they are too common."

He had come a great distance to trade. He secured what he wanted and, as I had a few knives left, asked for one of them. In exchange he took five fox pelts from his bag and gave them to me.

"You are mistaken," I said. "A knife does not even cost as much as one fox!"

He smiled in his mild way: "I am sorry. My tongue is going to protest against a white man. Perhaps it may fall out, but nevertheless I am right and must speak. You cannot know that I have been without a big knife for a whole year and have been missing it terribly. That is why I give you so many skins."

We continued our discussion in our house. In line with Eskimo logic, goods possess a value according to the need of the buyer rather than the scarcity or abundance of the supply.

"A thing may have no value," he said, "but I need it, and I pay for what I need."

I could not make him understand me. His idea was to let the purchaser decide the price. Many others said that they would certainly have appreciated their goods more if they had been more expensive—a psychology which some of our modern, fashionable stores realize to be sound.

6

When the time came for our spring hunting campaign to Saunders Island, offshore at Thule in North Star Bay, Knud stayed at home with his four old witches, Vivi, Arnajark, Semigak and Aloqisaq, to draw material for his book from them. Each of the women vied with the others in the telling of tales. Knud gave them little presents for their information—old tins, tea leaves, rags, and papers—and they stowed away whatever was left over from the table. Each woman collected these treasures in a box; when it was filled no power on earth could prevent her from setting out to distribute her gifts among her relatives. Knud could therefore determine from the amount in the boxes when the different women were about to set out on their journeys, and he extracted information frantically while he could, even though it meant passing up the hunting season.

It was at Saunders Island that I got my first walrus. I

had been out in a kayak numerous times and was anxious to get one, but never had the opportunity. Now it was my turn, and I was lucky enough to be directly behind the beast when he came up for air, so I rushed ahead.

Never had any animal looked so enormous to me, but I could not turn back without looking ridiculous. I remember that I even hoped it would hear the splashing of my oar and dive, but that was not to be.

I was almost upon the walrus before I had any plan in mind. It was breathing deeply, preparing to go down again. Now was the time. Suddenly my harpoon flashed through the air. Without waiting to see whether it had struck home, I whipped my kayak around and made off.

And the first thing I knew, men were shouting and hailing me from the other kayaks. I had got my first walrus!

I was "newborn in the land"—as the natives put it—because harpooning a walrus is the first step toward becoming a hunter. I was *somebody* now. The Eskimos even have a special word for "killing the first walrus," so important is that event in the life of a man.

All of us went back to the mainland to celebrate, and Knud, apparently scenting a party, arrived with his four ladies on his sledge. He had brought coffee and bread (he had actually planned on giving the party to celebrate the completion of his book, until I stole his thunder). But none of us cared about a book when such an important event had occurred: I had caught a walrus!

Knud Rasmussen returned to the house with the four old hags, and I stayed on the beach to collect eggs and catch more walrus. One morning I was aroused by an ear-splitting yell. Everyone was apparently going crazy, shout-

Top: Thule Eskimos cutting up a walrus.
Bottom: Head and skin of the same walrus.

ing and screaming, dancing and howling. What they were saying I could not ascertain, but finally I heard the word "Oomiarssuaq!" and a few moments later made out the masts of a ship sailing around Cape Atholl.

A ship at this time of year was totally unexpected. It was gradually approaching, and I induced the natives to wait until it was near before we set out. I must admit that the sight of its masts against the snow and ice was a welcome one to me.

Captain Adams of the *Morning of Dundee* was a veteran of the northern seas. Beside him on the bridge stood his seventy-four-year-old first mate. He had lived on a whaler for sixty years, and had never spent a summer at home since he was fourteen.

The two men were delighted to see me and pleased to learn that Knud and I had settled down at Thule. It was fine to go down into a warm cabin and have the steward serve me a meal that included bread and chocolate and sugar and hardtack. Captain Adams had brought mail for us, and I chatted with him for a long while.

Knud and I spent the evening reading our mail. I read letters from my family over and over again. They were filled with local gossip and warmth and affection, and I felt as if I were no more than a few miles from them.

I saved the letter from the girl I had left at home until last, partly to tantalize myself, and partly because I feared the news it might contain. I had not dared ask her to share my present life, yet secretly I had hoped she would. When I finally opened the letter, I could have cried with joy— she was coming up to join me, probably on the boat that was to bring us fresh supplies this summer!

Top: Knud playing host at the coffee feast.
Bottom: A native hunter in his kayak waiting
for seal or walrus.

She wanted to share my life, whatever it was. She wanted to live in my house, wherever it was, and become an Arctic woman. Together we would make life gayer and pleasanter than it had ever been anywhere in the world! I was in the clouds, and set about making preparations for her arrival.

As a letter from Knud's wife told him that he was the father of a newborn daughter, both of us were so excited that we scarcely knew what we were doing.

But while we waited for the boat we had to keep up our daily tasks. Summer came. We hunted in kayaks and traveled to near-by communities. One day during that summer Knud gave me the fright of my life.

We were after narwhales, which are amazingly fast. Knud was persistent to a fault, and when one came up on the left side of his kayak he threw his harpoon into the animal, though he knew that the whale should have been on his right side. When the whale dived it pulled the line attached to the bladder round Knud's body, capsized the kayak, and hurled him into the water. He was an excellent swimmer, but the line was twisted about him, and he disappeared below the surface in the wake of the wounded narwhale. The rest of us sat in our kayaks, absolutely helpless. For once I knew what it meant to feel my blood run cold.

After an interminable interval Knud came up far away, gasping for help. We rowed frantically, but long before any of us reached the spot where he had appeared he was down a second time. I was afraid he was done for this time, but a second later he bobbed up again. This time he stayed up and we hauled him out of the water. He had

Two views of the house at Thule—summer and winter.

hung onto the bladder, he said, as he figured his weight would quickly tire the narwhale and the animal would come to the surface.

"You'd better go home for a change of clothes," I said.

He eyed me reproachfully. "Don't you see that this is our chance for a big killing?" Later on I asked him if he did not at least want his clothes wrung out.

"Why?" he said.

"Because you're wet as hell!" I roared.

"By God, I forgot that!"

That's the kind of man who makes a real explorer.

The ship I had been so eagerly awaiting did not arrive. The harbor at Thule usually remained open for only twenty-five days each year—from August 1st to 25th—and already it was the middle of September. We were nearly out of supplies, especially matches and nails, and had to do something to replenish our store before the winter closed in on us.

One day on the way out to Saunders Island to pick up supplies from the cache of walrus and game I had left there, we saw a small schooner already there in the harbor. It was our ship; it had spent forty-five days in crossing Melville Bay!

My girl was not on it!

For me that was all that mattered. Born a lady, and reared in a large city, she had decided at the last moment that she could not face such an existence. I had known all along that it was asking too much of her, and I could not blame her for changing her mind. But at the time it was the worst blow that had ever hit me.

The captain of the boat said he could not stay with us one hour more than was absolutely necessary, so we pitched in and worked night and day at unloading. The ship was small and our money was low, but our credit was still good and we determined to stick with the career we had chosen.

I hastily dashed off a letter to my mother—the only one I had time to write. There was in it nothing of the thrilling stuff one reads in adventure novels. I had neither time nor inclination to worry her with that. And then the ship sailed away.

It would be difficult for outsiders to understand that we were glad to see it go, but we were. We settled back into our routine of living, and found it satisfactory. We slept two days and then decided to set out southward for bear meat.

At Cape York we ran across Minik, a boy who had caused us a great deal of trouble soon after we first came to Thule. He had been absolutely destitute when we first saw him. We had taken him into our house, where he was a great nuisance to all of us. He was an unhappy lad with a bad disposition. As a boy he, with his father and four others, had been taken to America by one of the American expeditions. All except Minik had been stricken during an epidemic in New York and died. He had been adopted by very decent people and been given every opportunity, but he was a born good-for-nothing. He felt that rules did not concern him, and laws were made for him to disobey. After countless attempts to get him interested in something—anything—he was given the opportunity to choose a profession. His choice was to steal money and run away.

He was apprehended at the Canadian border, sent back to New York, and finally brought home to Greenland on one of Peary's relief ships. He returned to the North with no property or money—he had been given plenty in America but had spent it all during the trip for liquor and such.

Minik had left us and was now living at Cape York in one of the houses reserved for the young people of the community. He wanted very much to marry a lovely young lady whose name was Arnanguaq, but he had no house. If he might move in with us at Thule, he said, he could offer her a shelter for the winter, and in the spring build her a home.

We thought it over and decided to let them move in with us—thereby saving Minik, who was probably a good enough fellow and only needed a break. Minik left for Thule the next day with his bride.

After a few days, Knud decided to go on south after more bear meat, but I had had enough of the trip and started for Thule alone.

When I reached home, I saw Minik working at last, adjusting to conditions and trying to make a living for himself and his wife. He had exaggerated his own importance, he said, when he was one of six selected to go to New York, and had been the only one of his people to survive the journey. But now he promised to begin over again and forget the outside world.

He and I built a small house beside our larger one. I moved in with him and his wife, as, in the Arctic, it is difficult to separate night from day and the natives are apt to run in at all hours to talk. Knud could stay up for twenty-four hours and then sleep almost as many but I liked to go to bed at a regular time, so I decided that our old house would be office, dining room, dwelling, and trading post. Knud would sleep in the attic when he returned from his hunting trip, and I would stay with Minik.

Minik's wife was not, unfortunately, much of a house-keeper. Her patience was inexhaustible, and there was not one ounce of bad intention in her. As a matter of fact, there were very few intentions of any sort in Arnanguaq, for she was as resourceless a girl as I have ever met. She could never think of anything to do. It was not long before Minik began to remain longer and longer away from the house on his hunting trips.

One day he announced to us all that he was going north, and he was going alone. He did not know how long he would be gone. I made no move to prevent his going and he set off, leaving me alone with his young wife.

To circumvent any whisper of scandal Arnanguaq in-vited Mequpaluk, the step-daughter of Uvdluriark, to spend the nights with her. Each evening after the girl had done all her chores at home she came running down to the house. Her clothes were disgraceful, her boots almost soleless, and her stockings furless. But she was always in the best of humor and our house became a gayer place when she entered it. She had a trick of recounting her experiences so quaintly that everyone laughed with her, and each night we awaited her arrival with impatience.

Finally one evening when she came, Arnanguaq was absent, and I told her that she had better stay with me. She looked at me a moment and then remarked simply:

"I am unable to make any decisions, being merely a weak little girl. It is for you to decide that."

But her eyes were eloquent, and spoke the language every girl knows regardless of race or clime.

I only asked her to move from the opposite side of the room over to mine—that was all the wedding necessary in this land of the innocents.

The next evening my little wife asked me to come down to the shore with her so that we could talk alone without a roof over us. She said that she had spent the day in speculation, and she had decided, now that she was married to a white man, to use one of her other names. She had been too frightened, however, to change her name without consulting me.

I agreed that she should take another name, and from then on she was known as "Navarana" over all Greenland.

As soon as Knud returned and learned of the wedding, he wanted to celebrate it with an enormous party. Much to the disapproval of the Eskimos who consider such a matter a private affair, Knud's will prevailed, as it usually did, and the festivities lasted for several days before Navarana and I could settle down to the business of living together our daily life as a young married couple.

Knud had brought with him the lame man, Tatarat, and his mother. I protested vainly that our house, where Navarana and I were now living, was already overcrowded, but since I had added to its congestion with a wife, my protests bore little weight. Besides, Knud needed the poor man to furnish him material for stories.

Tatarat had once been the most famous hunter in his tribe, but now his whole body was crippled. All his joints were stiff, and he could move only his jaw, and that with great difficulty. When he went on visits he was pulled

Navarana.

around by his old mother, who took care of him. He was always in the highest spirits and he was the best story-teller of the tribe. His useless limbs were withered and terrible to behold, but his mind was in perfect condition.

We had first met him at Natsilivik. We were with our host, filling ourselves on delicious whale meat, when we heard the dogs barking, which announced visiting sleds.

We ran out and shouted "Welcome," but among the shouts and cries reaching us from down on the ice was a voice which was cursing and raging most dreadfully. It was Tatarat's voice. We got the explanation later. They had been coming down the mountain slope to the settle-ment and his nephew, who was driving, had lost his grip on the uprights of the sled, which had then gotten away from him and overturned. Both his legs were broken, and he was furious, so furious that he could hardly think.

I recall asking him if his broken legs were giving him great pain.

"Oh, no," he said, "what do I care about my miserable legs that I can't even walk on! My legs have turned to wood, and wood can't feel any pain, but it drives me mad that that miserable fellow can't even drive a team of dogs properly. When I was that young I used to drive at full speed down that slope, and he can't even run behind and hold on to the uprights!"

Tatarat's mother left shortly on a visit to another fjord, allowing him to remain only on the condition that Knud personally would look after him. Soon the other residents of the house complained of Tatarat's odor, and it must have been high indeed to elicit comment from people who dress in skins and eat nothing but meat. Knud decided to give his friend a bath, and Tatarat made no serious objections. He had had, he said, many strange experiences, and he might as well try bathing for a change. I refused to touch him when I saw his body, which was not like a human body at all, but matted with long black hairs. Knud and Arnajark threw him into the tub and worked on him with brushes used, on pleasanter occasions, for scrubbing the floor. My only part in the whole thing was to carry away the water, which resembled a thick sauce. As his skin broke through the dirt, Tatarat's expression changed from one of surprise to delight. In later life he took several more baths and became a great propagandist for soap and hygienics.

Poor Tatarat also had other problems. His jaw became calcified. We had to pry his teeth apart with a piece of wood, which was very painful to him. But Knud figured out a solution. With a hammer he knocked out the man's two front teeth, upper and lower. We could then give him his food through the opening thus created, and also set the stem of his pipe in through the opening. His spirits were always very high. He was the local wit, and he knew all about scandals and never forgot anything, even the sayings of the little children.

Sometimes he would summon us with loud shouts of "I've lost my pipe! I've lost my pipe!" It would be lying an inch from his lips, and we would have to insert it again. He always laughed very heartily about this.

Navarana was almost as happy as she could be. She was easily the best dressed woman in the tribe. There was only one fly in the ointment: when certain women came to trade they recognized the skins they had traded to me in her garments, and they never neglected to tell her how happy they were at being permitted to furnish her with clothes.

This, of course, was not to be endured by any housewife, especially the wife of a hunter, and Navarana decided to trap her own foxes.

Trapping foxes had been a woman's job until Knud and I arrived among the tribe. The men could fight walrus and bears, and could hunt seals, since it takes great skill and strength to kill them. But now that fox pelts represented actual value, the men competed with their wives. The women, however, still had to procure skins for their own and their children's garments.

Navarana had already trapped a number of foxes, but had never before been permitted to keep the skins for herself. Now she had a team of her own dogs, and she visited her own traps and had great good luck.

Knud and I planned to make the trip to Tasiussaq that winter, taking Navarana with us. We had prepared a great many gifts for Christmas and I suggested that we postpone the voyage until after Christmas. We discussed it at length, but finally decided that postponing the trip so long might make our return to Thule rather dangerous, so we must set out early in December or not at all.

Nevertheless, we had our Christmas party—and a fine one it was, even if we did celebrate it on December 13th. Knud rigged up an artificial tree, and the natives were dazzled by its lights and colors. We invited everyone in the settlement, and everyone came. Each one accepted his gift with the utmost solemnity. The native missionary and his family were at first somewhat skeptical as to our wisdom in changing the date of the holy day. But when they understood that if they did not approve they would receive no presents, they realized that, so long as the church must be flexible, it might as well bend a little to the left at this time. We ate roast goose out of tin cans, and cakes, and sang all the Danish Yuletide songs. Navarana told me that, after this Christmas, she could never again pity herself. When there are such good times and such joy in the world, all other worries and troubles become insignificant details unworthy of discussion.

Knud and I suggested that, since the trip would be a cold one, Navarana should wear a man's costume. She was violently opposed to the idea at first, but when Knud assured her that in South Greenland the colony managers' wives all wore man's clothes, she finally consented. The man's costume is much warmer, consisting of a long coat and bearskin pants reaching to the knees. The woman's pants are made of foxskin and are much shorter. Their boots extend to the crotch, making walking difficult, and running almost impossible. The men wear a string of fox tails around their knees where boots meet pants to fend off wind and catch drifting snow. Secretly Navarana's friends laughed at her when they first saw her in a man's outfit, but later she told them how comfortable she was, and within two years all the smartest girls in the tribe provided themselves with such a traveling costume.

We set out shortly after our "Christmas," with the new moon. When we reached Cape York we learned that a great narwhale stake was in progress at Imnalugssuak.

Now a narwhale stake is the dream of every hunter, but it is so colossal a thing that no one dares speak of it openly.

Within an hour we were all racing toward Imnalugssuak. No one slept on the way down, and when we arrived we found the two small houses in the community jammed with people, and the excitement running high. The moon was brighter, and we left all of our women at the houses and drove out to the scene of the stake, about two hours away. On the way we passed great piles of meat and blubber, tusks and *mattak*. The natives had naturally taken as much meat as they could before sending the word to the surrounding country.

An entire school of narwhales had been trapped in the ice. A sudden cold spell had hardened the ice around the spot where they were feeding. At last there was so little space left that there was not enough room for all to breathe, and they crowded and shoved against each other when they came up for air, splashing water up over the edge of the ice and thickening it further, until they were complete prisoners.

They dived and swam as far as possible in search of another hole, but always had to come back for air. Every half-hour or more they came to the surface of the hole in great numbers, fighting and lunging about. It was not safe merely to shoot them, for the dead whales would be pushed aside under the ice shelf. We had to harpoon them and let them remain on the end of our lines until the school dived again. Then we could haul them up onto the ice and be ready for the return of the live ones. We could never tell in the darkness how many there were, but no matter how many we killed it seemed that just as many came back to the hole in the ice.

The poor animals had a bad time. They were not fright-

ened—a harpoon under their hide was as nothing compared to their air hunger—and it was almost an act of
mercy to kill them, since they would have strangled to
death or, had they come out onto the ice, been frozen.

We made a wonderful catch, finally refusing to harpoon the small ones but waiting for the bigger tusks to
appear. We collected hundreds in our store that year.

When I returned to the settlement I found Navarana
installed in one of the houses like the *grande dame* she
was. Later she told me that some of the older women—
among them a few of her own relatives—had been forced
to sleep outside on the sledges, and had complained. But
Knud had insisted that she sleep inside and never in the
future defer to her relations.

The rest of the trip was tiresome and uneventful.

At Tasiussaq, we were to stay with Knud's old friend,
Sören Nielsen and his Greenlander wife, who were the
social arbiters of the entire district. The Nielsens were
prepared for our arrival by runners who had gone ahead
to tell them of our coming. To my great surprise Navarana
was greeted with a certain aloofness, especially by Mrs.
Nielsen. Later I learned the cause of it:

The Nielsens had heard of me and selected me for their
son-in-law. Their daughter, Jacobine, was as yet unmar-
ried, and in Danish Greenland marriage is much more of
a business proposition than in the far north. Among the
educated natives and half-breeds the parents arrange the
marriages of their children, and the young people are
fairly content. They know they must marry young, or else
suffer the jibes reserved for spinsters and bachelors, those
ridiculous figures of Eskimo folklore. The entrance of the

bachelor or spinster is always the cue for laughter.

It took Mrs. Nielsen two days to get over her pique, but she soon became one of Navarana's closest friends. Until then she had been living in a splendid social isolation, as she was the only native woman in the colony who was married to a white man—now she could share this questionable distinction with Navarana.

Knud and I left Navarana with the Nielsens as we wanted to meet the district manager at Upernavik and inquire into the fate of a fellow explorer, Ejnar Mikkelsen, who we had heard had started for the Thule District via the north coast of Greenland and had never appeared.

The going was bad, as the water was swift between the various islands and wore out the ice from below. Our big sledges and heavy loads were a handicap in the south. We finally reached Kagsserssuaq and camped in a cave during a storm that night. Next day, we were able to go on.

In Upernavik we were the recipients of a brand of hospitality encountered nowhere except in the Arctic. The manager, Harries, and his wife could not do enough for us. It was grand to sleep in a bed between white sheets, and sit at table with white linen napkins on our laps. Every evening we danced, and the place rang with our shouts and laughter.

I remember that we asked the manager why he did not join us. He thought we were young jackanapes to be wasting our strength on such frivolity, and told us so. Later Knud took me aside.

"Peter," he asked, "do you think we shall ever be so old that we will not dance whenever we have the chance?"

At the time such a possibility was too remote for consideration, but in 1921 I reminded Knud of his remark. At that time a number of young fellows on an expedition stayed at our house in Thule, and asked permission to dance. We found it inconceivable that the boys wanted to dance every night.

Three pleasant weeks passed, and the ice would not freeze. As we were out of dog food and had to get back home, we decided to use skin boats to transport us across to the good ice. We were also determined, once we reached Thule, to set out in search of Mikkelsen. We bought some oatmeal (both of us hated it so much that we knew it would last a long while), and some solder to repair our stove.

We set out, and the water was as calm and free of ice as it would be in summer. Several of the natives accompanied us to bring the boats back.

One incident occurred en route to Tasiussaq which boded ill for the success of our venture. While rowing we sighted an object in the water—and, approaching it, decided that it was a sleeping seal. One of the natives had his harpoon ready before anyone else and hurled it at the very moment I discovered what it was. My shout was too late, and the harpoon struck the body—the body of a drowned man, Peder Lynge, a good friend of ours. He had gone out to shoot seals from the ice, and had worn new kamiks with slick soles. Apparently he had slipped and fallen into the water.

Now we had mistaken him for a seal and harpooned him—which, to a superstitious people, is worse than killing a man outright. The native minister refused to tell the widow, and we had to do so. The poor boy who had harpooned the body was told to cut off the handle of the weapon and leave the point in the dead man, and he was forced to give the stick to the widow to be buried with Lynge.

We were told that we had better give up all thought of the search for Mikkelsen. It was clear to everyone that we were not meant to go.

One day, as we picked our way across Melville Bay, on the last lap of the journey back to Thule, we saw the head of a bear high up on a towering iceberg. We stopped, and could scarcely credit our sight because there were no tracks leading up to the lair. We climbed until we could get a view, and found that there was a pair, a mating couple that had apparently been living on nothing but love for many weeks. It was impossible to drive them down to our level, so I, being the tallest, was chosen to scale the berg and shoot them.

Supported by the others, I chopped holes for my toes in the iceberg, and ascended as gingerly as I could. I was soon beyond the aid of my supporters and had to use my hands and feet to cling to the ice cliff. I reached the entrance to the lair and tried to maneuver my gun into position, but the male bear had no intention of permitting me to do this, and rushed me. He was so close that I felt as if I were in a cage with him, and I lost my hold on the ice and tumbled back onto the harpoon handles held by my friends. The bear above us retired to his cave.

We then decided that I should crawl back up with a rag fastened on the end of my harpoon with which to lure the pair out. This I did, and both bears charged the flag. Knud fired. I realized that I had no talent for playing the part of William Tell's son—the zing of the bullets was entirely too close for comfort.

There is an old superstition among the Eskimos that much evil will result from skinning and cutting up an animal on an iceberg, but there was nothing else for us to do as the bears retired to their cave to die, and it was impossible for us to get them out whole. The blood flowed like a brook and disappeared in a crack as we cleaned the animals. We hooked our lines around the carcasses and began to pull them out of the cave.

The moment we heaved on the meat there was a detonation like a cannon shot. It was all so sudden that I did not know what was happening. But the thunder rolled on and on. I felt as if I were treading air, and saw Knud tossed high above my head. Then I knew nothing until I recognized Navarana smiling down at me. Aside from a few minor bruises I was all right.

The iceberg, Navarana told me, had exploded, and we had all been hurled from it and out onto the ice below. I looked at the berg, and it was quite different in appearance, for it had tipped over, and was now bottom side up.

The explanation was simple: Icebergs are formed under terrific pressure within the icecap. When they slide out to sea and this pressure is removed, the slightest thing may alter their balance and throw them into violent readjustment. The warm blood of the bears flowing into the crack had done just that. As is so often the case, unreasoning superstition derives from an intrinsic truth.

The amazing thing was that none of us was hurt. The bears were half buried in ice, and our meat was much more accessible than it had been before.

We reached Thule without further undue interruption, and found a great many customers waiting to trade with us before we set out on our trip to locate Mikkelsen. We took care of them as best we could, and then began our preparations for the expedition.

~~~~~~

7

We were to take with us my father-in-law, Uvdluriark, and a fine young fellow, Inukitsork. They were the best men available and both volunteered to make the trip, not as hired men, but as Greenlanders whose unique privilege it would be to take a look at the other side of their country, and make their own observations.

We planned to follow the sea to the north coast, and then go east until we met Ejnar Mikkelsen, or came upon traces of him. We would return, well, when we returned. We might be forced to spend the winter on the other side, but what of that?

The day before we intended to leave I was called to a conference. Uvdluriark had been looking at the map, along with a number of the other natives who had been with Peary, and he thought it would be a waste of time to follow the coast around to the east.

"Why can't we go straight across?" he asked. "It looks as if it would be a short cut."

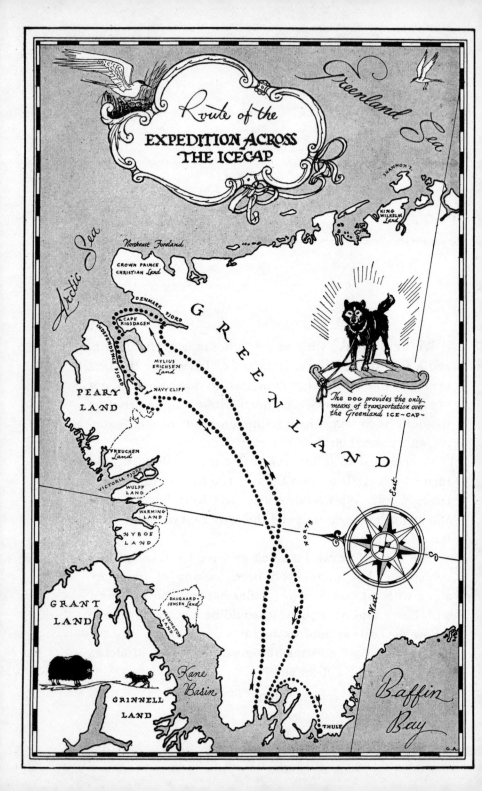

I tried to explain to him that such a course would lead us directly over the icecap—that we would encounter no land, and no game!

The interior of Greenland is covered by an enormous sheet of ice burying all valleys and mountains far below its surface. Its area is 727,000 square miles, and it is the greatest glacier of the northern hemisphere.

"The icecap is only a road without rough ice," Uvdluri-ark persisted.

We all talked it over and argued the possibilities. Then Knud joined the discussion, and asked me if it would not be possible.

There was nothing to prevent our trying it, except that we had insufficient provisions, no goggles to prevent snow-blindness, and we knew we would find no wild game until we came down on the other side.

"If you can navigate us across," Knud said, "we'll look out for the food!"

And so it was decided.

We started out on April 8, 1912, with thirty-four sledges, most of them loaded with meat, and three hundred and seventy-five dogs. Our plan was each day to send some sledges and drivers back as we gradually made room on our four sledges, by feeding our dogs, for the extra meat they hauled.

The first day we did not go far. Wise men of the tribe told us to ascend the icecap via Clemens Markham's Glacier—named for the old English admiral whose splendid explorations had been made near Nekri. The glacier was steep, and the humidity and heat were exhausting. The thirty-four sledges stretched back from us in a long, ragged column. The teams were eager to overhaul each other, even our own dogs who did not realize they had so far to go. We had used an old trick to advantage here—harnessing the bitches in heat among the forward teams; then the male dogs would haul any load in order to catch up with them.

A hodometer was attached to my sledge—a wheel that runs between the uprights and indicates the distance covered. It was scaled in kilometers, but it is impossible to travel in a straight line with dogs, and we could not figure the distance exactly. Nevertheless, it was better than nothing.

The glacier was surfaced better than any I had ever seen. It was slightly uneven in places, with a few boulders of ice caused by running water the preceding summer, but there were very few crevasses, and none large enough to swallow a man.

We did not feed our dogs the first night, so we had the whole crew with us another day. Next morning soon after starting out we reached a spot where the going was terrible. All the snow had blown off the ice, leaving no foothold for the dogs. We had to unload, drive on with half our loads, and return for the rest. Late in the afternoon we reached snow again and kept on until our dogs were exhausted. But by the third day there were only twenty-seven teams left, and we sent more home each day as our dogs consumed the walrus meat. After three more days we reached the interior dome of the icecap, and bade good-bye to all our helpers.

We were at last at the spot where the success or failure of the expedition would depend upon our speed. And our

Top: Ascending Clemens Markham's Glacier.
Bottom: Breaking camp on the icecap.

speed depended upon native methods, which no expedition of whites had ever used before.

The icecap is especially difficult to traverse because of the soft dry snow through which the runners cut easily. We had brought along from Nekri walrus hide sliced into long strips as broad as the palms of our hands. These we fastened beneath the runners of the sledges. Then we melted snow with our primus stoves and poured the water over the long strips, letting it freeze. It took us twenty-four hours to prepare the runners, but when we finished the sledges were almost as easy to shove as a baby carriage. With such runners much greater loads can be hauled over loose snow, and we had the advantage over sea-ice travelers that we could spread out our load without danger of its catching against ice hummocks.

At three o'clock on the morning of April 14, 1912, I took the hour angle, and we set out. Our course lay east-northeast, and it was no task to hold the direction so long as we could see the sun. Later on we shifted to northeast, so that we had the sun directly in front of us every morning when we set out.

Inside the icecap the snow drifts constantly. Even when one is unaware of the wind, dry snow sifts through the air covering everything, like flour in a mill. In no time the sledges were white, and the loads saturated with the stuff. We looked like ghosts driving ghost dogs. When we put our hands in our pockets we even encountered the snow dust there, and it was not very pleasant.

My special job, of course, was taking observations. So far as I was concerned I did not mind this task—at first. My talent made me especially valuable to the expedition, and

in the evenings when the others were cooking I could figure out my observations. But in the mornings it took me
a long time to get the hour angle, take the temperature and
pack my instruments, and do all those tedious little things
which are annoying for others to watch. They always drove
on without me. I had a number of bad frights when the
drifts had covered their tracks before I was ready to follow, and once, when they had gone far out of the pre-
scribed course, it was only by chance that I caught sight
of them through the valley between two drifts. Of course,
we all had enough common sense to realize that in case we
were separated, the only thing to do was to lie down and
wait for calm weather before we tried to find each other.

Knud's energy drove us on. Early every morning, while
we lay freezing on the ice in our sleeping bags and dreaded
the thought of going out into the cold and driving snow,
Knud would sing lively songs and ditties for us. He cheered
me up with the words and the Eskimos with his buoyancy.

Every evening, while we were building a shelter, he
would begin to heat water from snow in a little shelter
made of blocks of snow. One gets terribly thirsty up there
in the snow, and he would always give us the first luke-
warm water from the pot. We took our turn at the spout,
and only after we had slaked our thirst did he drink. Then
he would make tea, and the daily strife would begin, because he never learned how to make tea properly! I traveled with Knud for fourteen years, and I never had a cross
word with him except on these daily occasions. He thought
that tea should be *boiled*, and of course that's wrong.
Hence I got the first cup of tea, before he had boiled the
essence away, and he served the resultant slop to the

others. But in that way I got only one cup, and that annoyed me, because there was always enough for two cups for the others, who didn't care what they drank.

Until we reached the center of the icecap the wind was in our faces, but when we came to a large area in the very center there was no wind at all—apparently there is never any wind there; the snow was so soft that we could not cut it into blocks for igloos and had to use our tent. It was constructed of fabric not much heavier than bed sheets, but it lasted the whole time, and it served as a home for us during the summer. We anchored it in the snow and, even when it was really cold, we were so fagged out by night that we never again made igloos during the whole trip.

The dogs began to be unmanageable, and we had to resort to whips. We realized that they had to be fed oftener than we had planned on, and we saw our supplies running out faster than we had anticipated.

Our only hope lay in getting down to land where there were musk oxen before we had to eat any of the dogs; then we could find something for them—and us—to eat. But they grew lean, and so did we. We had overestimated our endurance, and there was nothing for it but to go on to the end.

The worst calamity of all—for all of us—was that I was slowly falling a victim to snowblindness. Unless a person has experienced it, he cannot appreciate the torture. Your eyelids feel as if they are made of sandpaper. Knud Rasmussen, who had much dark pigment in his eyelids, was not troubled, but I am rather light. Added to this, I had to take all the observations. Now that we were nearer land,

Knud and myself dressed for the icecap.

it was all the more important that we know our approximate position.

Finally a day came when I announced that tomorrow we would sight land. The icecap was now definitely dipping toward the sea, and the going was easy except for the snowdrifts. We were hardened against everything, cold and wind and pain, and there was in us only a concerted drive to reach land again—and fresh food. Suddenly I heard a shout and pried my eyelids open. There before us, between the drifts, were mountains! We were as happy as if we had found an unexpected cache of provisions. Now we had hard ice to drive on. We had no more use for our walrus-skin runners, so we took them off and chopped some up for dog fodder, saving the rest for ourselves.

Descending from the icecap is always more precarious than climbing onto it, for one cannot be certain what he will find at the foot. When we were close enough to the edge Uvdluriark went ahead to explore. We waited for him, I with my eyes closed and my coat over my head. He was gone for hours, but when he finally came back he said that he thought he had discovered a route down.

Once again we started the dogs, and this time the ice was so smooth and the slope so steep that the sledges ran up onto the dogs' traces. Knud's sledge ran over the neck of his left wing dog and killed it on the spot, but we could not even stop to pick it up and save it for food. There was no controlling the sledges, and I had to open my eyes regardless of the pain. The sledges chose separate routes down—there was nothing we could do to guide them—and I wondered whether we could stop them in time to avoid their crashing off the final drop onto the hard ice of a lake at the foot.

The wind was strong at our backs, and occasionally I caught a glimpse of my three mates whizzing along amidst a scramble of tumbling, snarling, yapping dogs. Then suddenly our paths converged in a kind of glacier river bed, and we all drew to a stop and unscrambled our dogs.

We looked about us, and found that we had stopped just in time. The glacier dropped in a perpendicular wall fifty feet to solid ice below—and there was no mattress to land on!

We tied our three harpoon lines together—it was impractical to detach the points from the lines as they were fastened on with leather stitches—and figured that they would reach the bottom. It was hard to get a foothold on the smooth ice at the top. We chopped holes to make it rough, and dug a couple of deeper holes for leverage. We also had to have a double line so that the last man to descend could, by a hazardous process, bring himself and the lines down together.

I was to go down first, since I was the heaviest. If the lines would hold me, the rest could descend safely. The idea was not particularly gratifying to me, but there was nothing else to be done.

A sealskin line is slippery and hard to grip, so I had to wind it once around my thigh. I lowered myself carefully over the edge, and started down as slowly as possible. Everything seemed to be going well until I happened to glance down. Within two inches of my thigh was the point of the second harpoon. I tried to grasp the line tighter with my mittens and hold myself up. I screamed, but they could not hear me above; even if they had heard me they could have done nothing. I had to make my way over the point somehow.

My hands continued to slip, and I felt the point penetrate my pants, and then my flesh. I kicked and finally got the loop free of my leg. But the harpoon point was already well into my thigh, and in coming out it tore a long, deep gash. It was over in a moment—I was rushing down now holding the line only by my hands—but I had time to realize that it must be rather unpleasant to be a seal. My swift descent was stopped when I struck the first knot below the point. I fastened the line round my leg once more and continued slowly to the bottom.

My entrance into the new country was not auspicious. I tried desperately to stop the blood with snow and my inner mittens. It was cold, especially with my pants torn and soaked with blood, and now added to the pain in my eyes was the sharp throbbing of my leg.

I could do nothing but wait for the others. They lowered the sledges and dogs, three at a time, but some of the dogs at the top grew panicky and jumped—beautiful flying arcs that ended in death. The men were the last to descend.

We chopped up more of the walrus-hide runners and cooked them for ourselves; then brewed some tea. We tied the dogs; the three that were dead we chopped up for their teammates. The dogs did not eat them at once, but next morning there were no signs of the carcasses.

Unfortunately I was now in such a state that I could do nothing. My eyelids were as thick as my lips, and I could only pry them open with my fingers. I could not walk

*The perpendicular wall of ice on which
I harpooned myself.*

without reopening the wound in my leg, and so there was nothing for me to do but lie quiet for a few days while the others explored the country and procured something to eat. They left one dog behind with me to warn me of bears or wolves.

All I wanted to do was to crawl head first into my sleeping bag and get away from the everlasting glare. I wanted no food but fat, and there was none. I wound my watches, but I did not look at them—I felt the need of complete relaxation for my eyes after nineteen days of observations on the icecap. We had actually traveled for only eleven days, but sometimes for more than twenty-four hours at a stretch; the rest of the time we had been laid up on account of storms.

As soon as I had recovered somewhat, Knud urged us on. He never lost his high spirits and was always the one who woke us every morning, or, rather, after we had slept the allotted number of hours. After all, it was light night and day so we could not observe the normal divisions of a day.

The dogs got steadily fewer and fewer in number. Some had died of exhaustion and two had been washed away by a raging river we had to cross.

After two or three days, they would go no further, and we were forced to butcher the poorest ones and throw them to their fellows.

Some days later we decided to cut the expedition down to three teams, using the fourth sledge for firewood. We butchered the four scrawniest dogs, and fed them to their teammates and ourselves. Dog meat is not too bad when the dog is young and fat, but ours were half starved and worn out with fatigue. Still, the meat was filling.

Next day we went out in scouting parties—Knud and Uvdluriark to the east, Inukitsork and I to the west. We shot a rabbit and ate it raw, but on the second day we returned to camp, realizing that this was no place to stay —no musk-ox tracks, no sign of big wild game anywhere.

Knud returned after four days with news that he had seen the sea. (He also brought three rabbits and six ptarmigans—he and Uvdluriark had eaten three of the latter already.) We looked at the map, and Knud was positive that what he had seen was Independence Bay, and the land across it, Peary Land.

If that were the case, then my calculations were incorrect. If we were only as far as Independence Bay, we had a long way to travel before we reached Denmark Inlet, and the country looked anything but promising.

Unfortunately Inukitsork had a touch of snowblindness, and we could not go on until he was better.

While we waited for him to recover I made sufficient observations to prove that we had reached Denmark Inlet, not Independence Bay. Our journey down to it, via what we named Zigzag Valley, had cost us more days and dogs than the whole journey over the icecap.

As soon as Inukitsork was fit to travel, we lost no time in moving on. The feel of the tough salt-water ice under us once more was good.

Soon we sighted signs of habitation on shore, and when we drove closer we discovered that it was actually the summer camp of Mylius-Erichsen, Hagen the soldier, and Jörgen Brönlund, Knud's old friend who, we later learned, had succeeded in bringing back the records of their explorations at the cost of his life. Their camp had been made in a most desolate spot. There was no game for miles around, and during the summer no possibility of getting away. Nothing to do but settle down to a lingering, horrible death.

Nearby they had burned a sledge—the ashes were still here. One of the iron runners was stuck in the ground to attract any travelers who might pass later. The dung of the dogs contained innumerable pieces of cloth, wood and rope, which indicated that they had consumed anything and everything. There were also bits of clothing.

The men had built a cairn, but there was no written message in it or any indication of where they had gone. Later on we learned that Ejnar Mikkelsen (the man we were looking for) had been here before us and had taken the script in the cairn without leaving any word of himself.

However, we assumed he had never been here and wondered whether we should go northwest in search of him at Independence Bay and the Peary Channel, or turn south along the east coast. Our equipment was equally inadequate for either venture. We decided first to head north, and rounded the northeast corner of Greenland—Cape Rigsdagen—named for the Danish parliament.

It is not a very conspicuous mountain, but I was determined to climb it, as it offered the only vantage point in the vicinity.

The coast looked none too inviting, so we crossed over to Peary Land. We had heard of this locality from the leader of the only expedition that had yet been there,

I. P. Koch, and we expected much of it. We were not disappointed.

From the sea we glimpsed a herd of grazing musk oxen —it is always a good omen for hunting when you sight game before touching shore. We pitched our tent again, and cooked a fine meal. Then we slept and three of us went out hunting while Knud stayed with the dogs and patched his underwear. He hated sewing for himself, but there was no one to do it for him, and I made fun of the picture he made sitting there with needle and torn garments slung over his knee. He took his revenge on me by using for patches the great blue handkerchiefs my mother had sent me.

We shot the oxen and had to make a number of trips to carry all the meat to camp. These remarkable animals are peculiar in that they never run away, so that one has to shoot the entire herd, because the living oxen remain to defend those that have been shot.

Our plan was to follow the coast down to the Peary Channel and then, if we did not find Mikkelsen, take it for granted that he had retraced his trail down the east coast. Later we learned that this was, indeed, what he had done.

As we progressed up the bay the ice changed from bad to worse. I made short observation trips into the hills at the side, and one day I came back to the party with some information which no one would believe: there was no such thing as a Peary Channel between Greenland and Peary Land. I had discovered that a glacier came down to the head of the inlet, and there would be no chance of our going much further on sea ice.

Knud and our Eskimo friends would not believe me.

Knud thought me an incurable pessimist anyhow, and besides, what Peary had said was good enough for him.

We went on up the bay slowly. It was now the middle of June and the brooks were swollen with water. There was no breeze to cool us off; the sun beat down ceaselessly, night and day. Our feet were sore, and the ice under us was a path of needles which bit through our soles. It was too warm at night to sleep in our bags, and we merely took off our footgear to try to get them dried. And they never dried.

The further we progressed the more evident it became that there was no Peary Channel—nothing but a high glacier awaited us at the head of the fjord.

Our dogs were in wretched condition, their paws cut by the sharp needles that form at the bottom of all the shallow ponds. We had to make footgear for them, adjust them every morning and take them off every night—if they are left on, gangrene is apt to set in because the tightness of the strings prevents adequate circulation.

We had eaten freely of our supply of meat, and the last few days had caught no seals. There were a number on the ice, but they were wild, and when we went after them we often had to swim across pools of open water.

There were twenty-five dogs and three sledges left. If absolute necessity faced us we could kill some of the dogs, eat them, and feed them to their teammates. We could last about a month in that fashion. The only thing to do was to try to hurry home via the glacier. If we got only one musk ox we thought the journey would be possible. Our immediate problem was to find an approach to the glacier, which we named for our friend Nyboe. Uvdluriark was elected to climb it and find a route back of it, which he did.

Before we ascended the glacier I tried to teach Knud how to secure the hour angle in case I should go snow-blind again. But he was a strange man. Possessed of a marvelous brain, he still had made up his stubborn mind that he could never learn how to do it. I tried to teach him, but we both got angry and gave it up amidst hearty laughter at our own sensitiveness. Then Knud celebrated the occasion with tea and pudding. Astronomy had always been a nightmare to him, and now he decided to give up its study once and for all. This, for Knud, was sufficient occasion to celebrate.

I remember the five days it took us to ascend Nyboe Glacier as the worst in my life. It meant pulling our heavy sleds thousands of feet up the side of the steep mountain. I had to admire Knud. I was bigger than he and could lift heavier weights than he could, but it was impossible for me or for any of the others to do what he did.

He carried his heavy sled in a sling which he fastened around his forehead, and got up to the top of the glacier without resting. This was a climb of seven hours, and when I arrived with my burden, which I had made lighter by twice loosening the sling and setting the sled down, I realized that I had found my master.

Our meat was gone, but we had to forge ahead, and our provisions consisted of fifteen pounds of oatmeal in an old pillow case. It could not be touched. It was our only reserve.

We wore holes in the soles of our boots and we wore out our neck muscles. But when we reached the top, Knud shot a hare which had recently borne young and therefore had milk in its udder.

"Sleep is milk, and milk is sleep!" was Knud's old motto, and we chewed on the udder and got the taste of milk in our mouths. And we went on.

A few hours later we shot some more hares, so many that we could give the dogs half of them, and we also shot some game birds for ourselves. At last we got across a foaming river and entered the Valmue Valley, where we rested.

Here were a great many musk ox, and we began to dry meat for the return trip; wonderfully fat ribs were laid out on stones, and, while we collected provisions and made observations, our stores increased and our dogs put on weight.

Tying our three sledges together, we continued on across rivers of ice. One day we encountered nine musk oxen. Knud and I had seven bullets in all. With these we managed to kill five. The rest were heifers, and we tried to scare them away. We were not successful, and then Knud got the idea to try his skill as a toreador.

I had a dagger which fitted into the barrel of a rifle, and with this weapon he killed the animals by charging them while I attracted their attention by throwing stones at them. I'll never forget Knud as a toreador. He rammed them precisely between the shoulders, and they fell dead at once.

As we returned to our tent we figured out that for two months we had eaten nothing but the meat of musk oxen, and then Knud said:

"If you could choose and could have anything in the world, what would you like to have for dinner tonight?"

"Well, I don't know; I really don't know. It's hard to say."

"What would you say," said Knud, "to a delicious piece of boiled musk ox meat? Could you imagine anything better?"

"No," I said, "not really." For that is how musk ox meat is, and that is how Knud was.

One morning Knud complained of a pain in his left leg. He limped slightly during the day, and when we packed meat I noticed that he carried less than the rest of us. That was not like him. In the evening he said he thought the pain had come from sitting on cold, damp stones, and he remembered that Harald Moltke had been ill all his life from sitting on cold stones as he sketched.

During the night he woke me up and said there must be a rock under his sleeping bag. I knew then that something was wrong; no man would wake a friend on such a slight pretext. He could not sleep, and he said that the worst thing that could happen to us was for someone to be taken sick. Somehow we had never taken this possibility into consideration.

Next morning Knud could not walk. He looked bad, and evidently ran a high temperature. There was no doubt that he had sciatica in a violent degree—caused by his having been wet the whole summer. Just as Knud Rasmussen always exerted himself more violently than anyone else in anything he undertook, so he was always sicker than anyone else when something was wrong with him, no doubt because his boundless energy kept him from giving in until he was absolutely forced to. He hated to be sick. But here in Great Wildland his pains were so fantastically great

129

that he lay awake for many days, biting a piece of hide in his pain. His concern for the expedition was not affected, however, and one day he told me that he considered it essential that I should return home. Since he was unable to travel, he would remain there over the winter with one of the Eskimos and would return to Thule the next spring.

However, we opposed him, and the decision was postponed for a week. But then he suddenly recovered to the point where he dared to undertake the return trip. We had only two sleds left, and thirteen dogs. I have rarely seen a face so twisted in pain as Knud's on that return journey. I went ahead on skis, then came Uvdluriark with Knud on the sled, using seven dogs, and behind him Inukitsork with six dogs. Knud lay on his back on top of the load, with his feet hanging out over the uprights, his face white as a cloth, his mouth pinched tight, and his eyes closed. Only when he got to an uneven stretch, where we all had to lend a hand in pulling the sled and it would bump and shake a great deal, would we see his eyes pinch a little tighter, but no sound would come from his lips. A couple of times the sled turned over, and he fell off. Then he would only say, "This is unpleasant!" so quietly and in such a way that we almost had to laugh at the incongruity of it all.

But fortunately he got better on the way. We made the trip in twenty-five days with quite a bit of difficulty, and when we finally reached the west coast near our settlement at Thule he was so strong that he made the last fifteen miles, which we had to cover on foot, faster than the rest of us. My feet were tender from many days of skiing, so that I fell behind, but when we reached the crest of the

*How I looked the day I returned from our
expedition across the icecap.*

last hill, from where we could see our houses, Knud was sitting waiting for us, and the four of us came down with our last five dogs; the rest had been killed for fodder.

And then there was feasting in Thule! All-night dancing and heavy eating! People came running with huge slabs of whale hide and rotten·bird meat and other kinds of delicacies, and Knud dissolved all of the journey's difficulties into laughter and gay stories. How the Eskimos grinned at the thought of our going hungry and carrying our sleds up the mountain while the meat of many walruses rotted in our cellar in Thule! And the women howled with scorn when Knud told of my clumsy attempts to resole our boots during the summer.

~~~~~~

8

Knud and I had come to believe that we had done something rather splendid in crossing the Greenland icecap by dog sledge. The feat had been accomplished only once before—by Nansen, in 1888—at a point much easier to traverse. And yet, far up north in Greenland, who was there to appreciate what we had done? Our trip had been unheralded prior to its advent, and unsung since its accomplishment. No radios broadcast our progress from day to day, no newspaper headlines screamed our achievement. No organizations offered us prizes, no cigarette companies sought us out to endorse their products.

We were both young and avid for recognition, and eager to bask in the spotlight after years of virtual isolation. We would go home to Denmark and let the world acclaim us!

That was a difficult year as far as ice conditions were concerned, and no ships got through to Thule. So we decided to set out across Melville Bay down through Danish Greenland to Holsteinsborg where we could board the first Danish ship to come in the spring.

We planned upon being gone only for a few months.

Navarana did not wish to remain in our house, and I proposed that she go with us as far as Tasiussaq and live there with the Nielsens until we returned.

That trip was full of adventure and fun, and we amused ourselves like two schoolboys on vacation. On Melville Bay we watched Knud track a polar bear on a newly formed ice floe, and they both fell into the water where Knud splashed around with the bear. He lost his gun, and it sank to the bottom. A Greenlander came running up, frightened out of his wits, and wanted to shoot, whereupon Knud gave way to a rare burst of anger and bawled him out like a Prussian.

"Do you really think that I take all the trouble to chase a bear for you, and fall into the water in the attempt, and then have a clown like you shoot it? Give me a hand and let me have your gun, and I'll show you how a bear is to be shot!"

The Eskimo was more frightened of Knud than of the bear, which was almost upon him, so he hauled Knud up out of the water, and there, with his feet still dangling in the water, Knud grabbed his rifle and shot the bear with one shot.

Later Knud got the idea that he no longer wanted to *shoot* bears. There was a matter of honor involved and a regard for the majesty of the king of the ice wastes, so he got himself a lance to kill the bear with after his dogs had surrounded it. I don't understand that sort of thing. I prefer a gun, as the bear hasn't got one, and at a certain distance I feel myself to be safe.

Along the way, we stopped at the place of a friend, a Greenlandic outpost administrator and a fine man. In the evening we sat at his table and drank tea. He didn't have much rye bread, which was the finest food on the table, so I therefore ate ship's biscuit. Knud, on the other hand, helped himself without stint to the rye bread.

Our host entertained us by telling us about his bleedings, and how best to stanch them, and he made the unexpected statement that he found dough to be the best remedy. As an explanation he told us of his experience.

"I always knead the dough for my bread myself," he said, "and I suffer terribly from warts on my hands. Every time I touch anything they bleed. When I begin to knead dough, they bleed pretty badly, but in a short time it stops completely. It's the dough that does it—help yourself to another piece of bread."

I sat and gloated about my ship's biscuit and told our host how Knud had been longing for bread. Knud protested in vain. He had to put away three more slices!

We arrived next in Pröven, where a great hunter called Little Jonas lived. Knud had first met him on one of his previous trips to Greenland and he was Knud's faithful friend. When visiting Jonas we never paid for dog fodder; it was ours in advance. Knud would never think of journeying by sled south to Umanak without taking Jonas along.

Between Pröven and Umanak there was a little hut where, in the summertime, travelers would pick up coal and oil.

Some bears had been there and had played games with the place. The chimney lay down on the beach, and Jonas was given the job of setting it up again. He put it upside down, and it was impossible to get the smoke out. Knud was the cook, and he sat in there undisturbed, preparing pancakes in a miasma that the rest of us could not stand. We had to rush outside in order to breathe. The cooking aroma and the delicious steam of burning fat wafted out the door, and we suffered the torments of Tantalus as we heard Knud singing gay songs inside while he turned the pancakes in the air so that they fell down with a smack.

"Come in and eat! Come in and eat!" he called out once in a while. But no other mortal could have breathed in there, and we never did eat those pancakes. We had to cook some meat for ourselves out in the cold.

Our longest layover was at Ikerasak, the home of Knud's Uncle Jens. Uncle Jens and Uncle Carl had always maintained a friendly rivalry, each trying to outdo the other in entertaining Knud.

Uncle Jens had even organized a choral union with only one duty—to sing songs when Knud visited the place. The club was sent for at three o'clock in the morning. Soon all its members were gathered at Uncle Jens's house, and hard at work. And how they worked! We had been traveling the whole day and I thought myself entitled to a few hours' sleep, but Knud instructed them to come into my room and serenade me. There being no opportunity for sleep, I got up and joined the celebration. Uncle Jens then decided that upon such an occasion no one should sleep, so he rushed about the village with strong coffee rousing everybody out of bed. Soon the house was filled with dancing couples, singing, and wrestling bouts.

In the middle of the feast Uncle Jens, overcome with love and generosity, threw open his store and gave the natives whatever he thought they needed. (I must explain

136

that next day all the natives came trudging back with these supplies and surrendered them gladly. They realized that the old man was moved to such an act by the presence of his well-loved nephew.)

It was only natural that the whole settlement should be fed and offered free coffee during our stay; as the generous host was unable to pay for it himself, the burden fell on Knud. Knud, being completely charming and generous, felt that the party was well worth the price and even sacrificed our entire supply of liquor for the festivities.

From there we drove across the hazardous "Majoren," the high pass between Umanak Fjord and Disko Bay, stopping to visit Uncle Carl at Qeqertak, but he was displeased because our whole supply of liquor had been drained by Uncle Jens's celebration, and we moved on south.

At Ritenbenk, where we slept in the clean beds of the post manager, we were awakened one morning by a stranger poking his head into our room. He was a young assistant post manager on his way from Godhavn at Disko Island to Egedesminde, where he was being transferred because of the former manager's death.

We knew immediately—we would have known anyhow without his telling us six times during the first half-hour— that here was an important young man indeed. He had heard, he said, that we were traveling south, and wouldn't it be much safer for all of us if we teamed up and went together? We assured him that it certainly would, and he seemed very pleased. As he was a government employee the natives would all obey him, he said, and we agreed this would take a great burden off our shoulders.

The young assistant was a rank newcomer to Greenland, and had with him as pilot a half-breed, Karl Tygesen, the Copenhagen-educated son of a former manager. Karl, because of his ever-ready humor, had never gone far up the social and official ladder. He was, however, eager for any joke, and assured us that the trip with the young man would be better than a circus.

As we drove on next day the royal assistant thought we ought to settle one thing now: Who would be the leader? We elected him unanimously.

After we had conquered the first hill he turned to us and asked if we had ever climbed such a hill before. Of course, we had not. Karl Tygesen then announced that he could not tackle the next hill without a stimulant. He was, he said, on the verge of exhaustion.

Our leader produced a bottle from a case on his sledge. The glass was filled twice and passed around. To drink on the trail, our commander said, was not his practice, but if we ate something with it he could permit this letting down of the bars. He brought forth cookies which his mother had sent him, and served them with jam. Then he graciously offered us much good advice about how to get the best out of our dogs.

After another stop, and another drink, we climbed the third and last hill. The bottle was empty now. Fortunately I never drink myself so I was able to drive ahead and take care of our leader, who was sound asleep when his sledge drew into the next settlement.

The next day bad ice forced us inside the usual route along the fjords, and this meant crossing more mountains with the help of more bottles and the cookie jar. We did not get very far, and had to stop over at the house of a hunter in Qilaussuaq.

The hunter's dwelling boasted two rooms, and we were assigned to the inner one. The hunter himself was an old friend of Knud's—he had been married in Knud's father's church—and was delighted to have some fresh seal meat to offer us. This, of course, was especially welcome to us as we had been eating nothing but delicious delicacies in the Danish houses.

Our leader and protector turned slightly green at sight of the meat, and asked us whether we had ever tasted seal meat. (It is not eaten by the better-class Danes in Greenland.) We said that a few years ago we had sampled it, and so far as we could remember, the stuff was edible. Karl assured him that it really was a sort of food, but could by no means be eaten unless accompanied by a glass of gin.

The young man hurried to fetch his bottle, and Knud, always the cook, proceeded with the preparation of the seal. He gave the assistant a generous portion, and we all ate ravenously—all but the assistant. After a few moments he timorously asked us if we minded his getting a tin of sausages and boiling them himself. He was sorry but he had only enough for himself and could not offer us any.

Knud graciously insisted on warming the tin, but unfortunately emptied the contents into the seal soup and boiled it in that fashion. The young man ate nothing but hardtack and coffee. Nevertheless, he was soon as gay as ever, and told us more about the land and the natives than we could ever hope to know.

For instance, one of his friends had seen—he could not guarantee this, but his friend swore it to be true—an

139

Eskimo eat the warm liver of a seal without cooking it. The poor friend had almost vomited. We all said this must be a lie, and under no circumstances would we believe it. But Knud secured the liver from the seal we were eating, and began to eat it before our eyes. The young man bolted.

We passed Knud's birthplace, Jakobshavn, which is the greatest source of icebergs in the world and soon reached Nordre Huse. Our leader was impatient with us, as we wanted to stay a while and talk with the natives, so he said he would drive on to Claushavn and there arrange for our accommodations with a Danish host.

At Claushavn our young friend had secured a separate room for himself and an adjoining one for the three of us. He had, however, planned without being aware of Knud's rule never to permit anyone to sleep when he wanted to dance. The house was an old log structure once used as a whaling station and fortification, and there was plenty of room to dance.

Several young people were invited, but unfortunately we had no refreshments to offer, and once more we had to resort to the young assistant's case of liquor. Not to make the donor too angry with us, Karl Tygesen refilled three bottles with water and restored them to the box. Later it occurred to the boy to do his share in the evening's festivities, and he went out to bring in a bottle. The three bottles had frozen and broken open. We assured him that the dealer must have furnished him with inferior liquor. Knud tried to cheer him up by telling him that the boys at Egedesminde would undoubtedly have taken the liquor away from him anyway. The lad soon became somewhat enamored of one of the native belles, so the evening was a great success.

At last we came to Holsteinsborg, and within a few days shouts rang over the village. The ship from Denmark was here!

It would be almost impossible to describe our emotions at the sight of a ship approaching us there in the wilderness, bringing with it news, good and bad, of our homeland. Before this one had anchored the sailors shouted to us that our King was dead; that our people in Denmark were worried about us; that Ejnar Mikkelsen had been rescued by a Norwegian seal hunter; and that it was known we did not possess the provisions to attempt the venture which we had, indeed, already accomplished. Prominent explorers had informed the public that it would be impossible for us to cross the icecap.

We hired two trustworthy boys to look out for our dogs and feed them twice a week while we were away, and then boarded the ship.

When we sailed we discovered that a sweet but feather-brained Danish girl had given up her job as a teacher to follow us to Denmark. She had heard from the captain and others that we would doubtless be feted and wined and dined because of our accomplishment. This, to her, was a thrill she could not afford to miss. Neither Knud nor I had been responsible for her coming along, but each of us suspected the other of an intrigue. As a matter of fact, both of us were innocent.

It was fine to be on the ocean again, and we nearly went crazy at the sight of the first ship riding the horizon.

Our ship, the *Hans Egede,* on which I had once been a

stoker, put in at the Faeroes and we decided to telegraph messages of our safe return from the icecap to all our friends. We walked straight to the telegraph station and secured a sheaf of blanks, the manager eyeing us apprehensively and asking whether we had the money to pay for them. When he saw that our first message was to the King, he sprang to attention like the loyal subject he was. We dispatched telegrams to the Geographical Society, the papers, officials all over the world, our families—and sent them all collect with no further objections.

The boat was boarded many times during the trip down to Copenhagen, and we were lionized by the publicity purveyors. At the harbor we were greeted by relatives and government representatives. Long and windy speeches were made, eloquent things were said of us, and tall glasses emptied. We replied as eloquently and evidenced our joy at being home—and then the prominent men went away.

On shore the girl from Holsteinsborg was my special burden, in spite of having a clear conscience about the whole thing. Knud, of course, had rushed to his home as he had a three-year-old daughter whom he had never seen. My dear mother looked at my human baggage as any mother would, but the girl had to be disposed of somewhere, so I put her up at a hotel.

It was delightful to be with my family, and I did not miss the acclaim we had anticipated until, after some hours, Knud telephoned and asked me if I happened to be busy that night. When I replied that I had no definite plans, he said:

"Well, it wouldn't be you and me if we didn't do something. It doesn't look as if anybody is going to do anything for us, so we'd better do it for them."

We scurried about and sent invitations to all the prominent men, and many others, for a big party in our own honor at the best hotel in Copenhagen. Always a little more cautious and prosaic than Knud, I asked who was to pay for it.

"You and I," he said. "If we crossed Greenland and came back alive, it would be too bad if we couldn't tackle this!"

Such a party! A few of the prominent citizens actually turned up, but Knud stole their thunder. Dressed in the costume of our icecap expedition, he bewildered everyone by leaping onto the table and delivering a speech of welcome to the guests whom we had longed to see for three years. Then he organized dances between the different courses, and the maître d'hôtel hurriedly snatched away the more expensive china.

The party was later referred to as the greatest event that had ever struck Copenhagen, and our little schoolteacher was wide-eyed with wonder. As the evening progressed Knud ran down to the hotel restaurant and recruited more guests from among the late diners. We had returned home expecting to be feted; if no one would fete us, we would make up for their thoughtlessness.

But next day we were abandoned again, and I remember Knud and myself walking the streets in the evening and comparing our reception with those tendered the much publicized expeditions which had gone out with government support. Even Arctic explorers need publicity.

Apparently we were not much in vogue at that time. We

saw in the papers that various Geographical Societies throughout the world had interested themselves in what we had done, so we applied to the "Carlsberg Fond," a famous scientific institution in Denmark, for $700 to cover the cost of our expedition across the icecap. The sum was, after all, trifling, and the members of the dignified institution felt a bit embarrassed at giving us the money which, after a great deal of haggling, they finally did. However, they advised us to apply for more next time as most people would think that nothing of any great importance could be accomplished with only $700.

In reality, of course, Knud and I felt that we had accomplished something extraordinary and that the world would want to pay us tribute. We had arrived home at a bad time, however. The day we visited the Prime Minister he handed in his resignation. Our trip to Denmark had been, as a whole, disappointing. I longed to go back to Navarana and the cold North.

Knud, however, had begun to write immediately. His home and his two lovely little girls, Hanne and Inge, quieted his wanderlust for a while.

I remained at home for only five weeks, and sailed for Greenland once more through the kind offices and faith of Mr. Nyboe.

Now that our trading post was established, Nyboe bought us a little ship, the *Cape York,* and secured for it the best captain in those waters, Peder Pedersen.

The plan was for me to sail ahead on a commercial vessel with Ajago, an Eskimo boy who would be part of the crew on the *Cape York.* We would land at Ivigtut in South

Greenland, purchase the supplies we would need and there await our ship.

But in the meantime the *Cape York* was delayed. I later learned that its motor had broken down completely. When our ship failed to arrive, I decided to go on north to Thule. I did succeed in getting part of the way north by motorboat, but my progress was rather slow, and I had only reached Egedesminde, halfway up Greenland's coast, when I was aroused one night by a number of girls squealing inside my room. Half asleep, I chased them out, but one, whose voice was louder than the others, shrieked that Knud was outside.

"What Knud?" I asked. I knew that my Knud was far off in Denmark with his wife.

"It is Knud! Your Knud!" they shouted, and, suddenly awake, I rushed down to the pier. The nights were already dark, but in the harbor I saw a motorboat and in it Knud Rasmussen!

Knud had heard in Denmark that I was marooned at Ivigtut waiting for our ship to arrive, and he had worried lest it arrive too late, after the water had frozen over. He had jumped on a steamer bound for Ivigtut, expecting to find me there and plan with me some course of action. At any rate, he had wanted to be with me if I were having difficulties. He had reached Ivigtut at the very moment that the explorer J. P. Koch had arrived there in his motorboat to embark for Denmark.

Playing in luck, as always, Knud had purchased the motorboat and followed after me. Just outside Ivigtut he had encountered our ship, its motor disabled beyond repair, and had taken Captain Pedersen into the harbor at

Ivigtut to purchase sails for him and gone back to the ship to collect Pedersen's engineer, who would be of no further service on a motorless vessel. Knud then towed the *Cape York* outside the fjord, and Pedersen proceeded with the cargo to Tasiussaq.

Knud's motorboat was a beauty, designed along the newest lines. We left at once for Godhavn. On the way we sighted the *Cape York*. It was becalmed, its sails hanging limp and lifeless, so we took it in tow and progressed slowly for several knots until a gale struck us, the sails billowed, and we had to cast loose in a hurry or be run down.

We arrived in Tasiussaq, where I was to pick up Navarana, and finally the *Cape York* arrived. We towed it in with the motorboat, landed its cargo, and then sent it back, although it was late in the year.

It was a question whether the *Cape York* could even return to Denmark without a motor, but Pedersen swore he would not spend the winter in Greenland. We towed him out of the harbor and waved good-bye to him in the dark. When we left him the snow was already sifting down, but he hoisted his flag in salute, and sailed for home. They had a difficult trip, we learned many months later, and did not reach Denmark until late in January, 1914.

Now the problem was to get our goods transported to Thule. I would have thought it impossible, but Knud looked upon it as a game. We decided to transport the load in shifts by motorboat as far as the ice would permit —up to Björneborg, a little island in the southern part of Melville Bay.

On one such trip we were driven by a storm far out to

Top: Our new motorboat.
Bottom: The Cape York.

sea and it was several weeks before we got back to Tasiussaq.

One poor Greenlander named Polo, who was with us, suffered the unhappy lot of finding after we got back that his relatives, thinking him dead, had divided up his belongings among themselves, and that his wife had been taken over by his brother. She was the only thing he got back, since the heirs refused to return what they had inherited and had, in part, already sold.

On the last trip Knud and Ajago and their dogs remained in Björneborg, while I went back to Tasiussaq with the motorboat. I was never told of their adventures there, but when I got back over the ice there were twenty-two bear skins beautifully salted down, great stores of meat, and half a barrel of salmon. They had taken off northward across Melville Bay and had collected forty sleds, which soon came down to transport our goods up to Thule.

~~~~~~

9

When we got home to Thule we heard that an American expedition under MacMillan had arrived at Etah, at the extreme northwest corner of Greenland. This was a source of pleasure as well as trouble and adventure. We had to face the situation of having other white men in the Thule district. In the first place, they would keep many natives busy and away from their normal pursuit—fox hunting. Second, the American market for fox pelts was excellent, and these men could easily compete with us since their expedition was financed at no cost to the men themselves. Their supplies might also prove to be more desirable to the natives than ours. At least, they would inevitably be different, and that would make them desirable for a time.

The night after our arrival Dr. Elmer Ekblaw of the American Expedition called upon us. We hadn't eaten anything the day he came because among all the things we had brought back to Thule we had not brought food.

We had only a rotten piece of walrus meat. I said to

149

Knud that we should ask the American to bring his own food in.

"Not at all," said Knud, "I'll take care of it!" And he went out to our guest and stretched out his hand as if welcoming a king.

"What a great pleasure it is to welcome you, particularly today, because we are fortunate enough to have in our house a piece of slightly putrid walrus meat with a rare scent. It is a great pleasure to be able to offer it to you."

It developed that Ekblaw had never tasted rotten meat as the Eskimo eats it. "It is a pleasure twice over for me," said Knud, "to be able to be the first to serve you this delicacy."

The stinking, frozen meat was carried in by two men, and Knud took an axe and chopped it up expertly. He sought out the most "delicious" piece for Ekblaw and laid it before him.

"I am giving you an especially good piece of strongly smelling meat; it has had neither too much nor too little of the summer's heat." He became quite eloquent in his joy over his guest's good fortune, and Ekblaw got it down only with considerable difficulty.

"You will not deny that this is a rare treat," said Knud. Ekblaw answered, "No," and Knud beamed.

"Oh, how wonderful it is to have guests who appreciate one's offerings. You must have another piece!"

"Oh, no, no, thank you," said Ekblaw, "no, no, I've had plenty!" But Knud overruled him: "Let's not have any modesty! We live in a place where guests come rarely and are doubly welcome!"

A huge piece was laid before Ekblaw. Knud entertained

him with gastronomical adventures. When Ekblaw had swallowed the last piece he was blue in the face, and Knud continued his prank.

"You know," he said, "we Danes usually top our meal with coffee, but I'm sure you'll admit that it would be sheer vandalism to spoil that walrus's fine aroma with coffee and to mix a tropical drink with this Eskimo delicacy. No, only clean water, melted glacier, should be taken after this course!"

I breathed easier, because I had stiffened as soon as I heard him mention the word "coffee." Whatever we owned of that commodity was hundreds of miles away.

But the next morning Ekblaw anticipated developments and offered us some of his travel provision, of which he had a plenty.

When he got back to Etah, he reported that he had been entertained so royally and received so heartily that the trip had been richly rewarding.

We still had at least fifty additional loads of goods to bring up from the south, and the only way to accomplish it was to convince the natives that the hauling was little more than a pleasure trip for them. Knud was the man to arrange this.

Those who had fox skins to sell were asked to deliver them to us and then go south and pick up their goods at Tasiussaq. They could easily bring back a few boxes, and Knud told them that they had such fine dogs that he was eager to see how much they could haul. They would also be able to feed their dogs from his meat at Björneborg, so that the journey would in the end be a saving.

We traveled back and forth, back and forth. No longer

were we hunters or adventurers, but freighters and haulers, and this took away much of the excitement of crossing Melville Bay. The anxiety of driving tired dogs through the darkness, the snowstorms, the everlasting cold, was disheartening. Melville Bay was a highway that winter, and the natives grew as weary of it as we did.

But Knud Rasmussen blossomed under the grueling routine. I can still see him standing in the middle of Melville Bay, the going bad through deep snow or rough ice, the dogs balking, the Eskimos disgruntled, no dog food, no fuel or provisions, and home far, far away. Then he was gayest and most at ease. He loved to manage people, to praise some, scold others.

When everything that could be transported had been brought to Thule, Knud Rasmussen drove back south and took a ship to Denmark. Meanwhile, I remained and prepared for a trip to Peary Land, but nothing ever came of that. On April 15, 1915, just before I was to take off on that trip, a sled arrived from the south with a letter from Knud, written in August, 1914, and sent northward along Greenland's coast through extraordinary arrangements. The letter told me that Europe was at war, "a terrible war," wrote Knud, the like of which no one had ever seen and the extent of which was difficult to fathom. "Yes, pessimistic men even maintain that it might last until October, although it is hard to believe that such mass murdering will be tolerated that long. But inflation will come," wrote Knud, "so please take good care of your things and explain to the people up there that this fall the world is experiencing the greatest fright in its history."

And he also told me how the war had progressed. During the last few days great numbers of Russian troops had been sent to northern England and would be used to help drive the Germans out of Belgium. The outcome of the war was thus assured.

I went to Etah immediately and told the American expedition there about my latest news, and then we sat down, as one always does in Greenland, and conducted the war and European politics, but we didn't hear any more about it for a long time. No ship brought tidings, for everything was at a standstill. However, we got along, and even though not well at least well enough so that no one starved to death. We had, to be sure, a rather hard winter, and the ice simply did not break up during the summer. There was a shortage of meat everywhere, but this was a want which was common to us all.

The Eskimos, however, were convinced that the abnormal weather and other conditions were due to the fact that the world was ashamed because human beings were acting like wild animals. The world, therefore, did not wish to be as friendly as it usually was. The old men held séances but could accomplish nothing, and they thought that most odd.

"We know that Knud is down there in the white man's world, and he usually manages to set things right no matter what is wrong," they said.

I tried to explain what was involved and managed to elicit a certain amount of understanding. Some of the tribe's older and wiser men came to me and said that if only a ship would arrive, they would send ten or twelve of their young men down there, armed with rifles, and place them under Knud's command so that they could break the white men of their habit of using ammunition to kill each other.

No ships got through to the American expedition at Etah either, and I drove three of their men across Melville Bay down to Danish Greenland, so that they could get home.

When I got back from my trip with the Americans, all of the people were put on rations. Each household got two boxes of matches a year, and each hunter thirty bullets. I went hunting on Saunders Island, stored up depots of walrus meat, collected eggs for winter fare, and laid out eider ducks to rot.

Then one night, when spring was just beginning to show itself, we heard shots. The boys, we thought, must have sighted a bear, because ammunition was scarce and they would not be wasting it. We considered it for a moment and then went to sleep again. But not for long. Again we were awakened by gunfire, and I decided to go home and find out what it was about. We could expect no ship—I had heard that in South Greenland—and all this powder was apparently being wasted.

It was not a ship, but a familiar, heart-warming figure— Knud Rasmussen! He stood there on the shore, waving his arms at me in greeting. He had come up to Greenland on the first boat permitted through the North Sea.

Knud had been in London, had seen wounded soldiers and men on furlough, and had then felt a need for action well up in him. He wanted to get out again and up to Greenland with the first ship in the spring. Lauge Koch, a young student who later became famous as a geologist and Arctic explorer, came with him, and the two of them

Top: Lauge Koch.
Bottom: Knud entertaining a group of natives
at the house in Thule.

had managed to get up to Thule by sled and boat. They slept only while riding on the sled, and they used every contrivance and trick possible.

~~~~~~~~~~~~~~~~~~~~~~~~~~~~~~~~~~~~~

10

Europe, Knud told me, was still in the grip of war.
Denmark was one of the few neutral countries. For Knud,
reading of the other nations at war, the strain of enforced
idleness was too deadly, so he and Koch had decided to
come north and try to accomplish a mapping expedition
up the north coast. Knud had to postpone that until fall,
however, as the dogs were in too poor shape.

Life again settled into a routine. We did almost no
hunting that summer, and I occupied myself by writing
a great deal.

One night I fell asleep after having written for a number of hours. Navarana had gone down to the tents, which
the natives lived in during the summer months, to eat
mattak, as two narwhales had been caught that day. I had
been invited, too, but for some reason or another I had
not gone.

In the middle of the night she came home complaining
of a stomach-ache. We thought it nothing more important
than eating too much *mattak,* and she went into the other
room and to sleep.

A few hours later Arnanguaq, who still lived in our house, came to me with the news that Navarana's time had come—she was going to give birth to her child.

I was frightened half out of my wits. I had realized, of course, that this moment would arrive sooner or later, but we had not known when the baby was due. I cried to Arnanguaq to look out for Navarana, and I bolted out to call Knud. He came running and was as bewildered as I.

"But anyway," he said—by then he had two children and was therefore an authority—"let's go for water. They will need it."

We went for the water, as I knew it would be a long while before the actual birth took place. When we returned the boy was already born!

I had to let everyone know at once, and ran shouting from house to house.

The boy had been born at 3 A.M., June 16, 1916. At eight o'clock that morning Navarana got up again, straightened her house and walked out with the boy on her back. At five o'clock that night she led the celebration and danced with abandon. She went to bed, however, before all the guests had departed, complaining of being tired.

The boy himself was a healthy specimen. One of his eyes had a slight cast, but everyone knew that this misfortune was only to assure us that he was really old Mequsaq—Navarana's one-eyed grandfather—reborn. He also possessed a blue Mongolian spot at the base of his spine, as does every Eskimo child. This would fade by the time he was three or four years old. But in addition, there was another birthmark farther up on his back, near his kidney. This would seem to indicate that he was also to be named

"Avatak." A boy of that name who had lived up north had just been shot by his uncle in a fit of hysteria. The bullet had entered the body at the same spot as the mark on our son. Thus the boy entered the world with names already provided.

As fall came on, it seemed fairly certain from the look of the ice in Melville Bay that no ship would be able to reach us that year. But just as we were about to give up hope, we sighted a boat and went almost mad with joy!

The ship brought wild tales of dangerous ice and more news about the war. We were told by the captain that supplies had been sent to us but that the steamer transporting them had been sunk by German U-boats.

On board were a number of passengers, among them Dr. Torild Wulff, a Swedish naturalist and student of marine life. He wanted to collect specimens of vegetation at Thule.

Dr. Wulff asked if he might move in with us, and I consented, since Knud and Lauge Koch, who usually slept in our attic, were planning to spend the winter in Tasiussaq with the Nielsens. Besides, Dr. Wulff had brought along his own food. He was not, however, fit to consort with the Eskimos. He had recently been in China, and he loved to tell how he had once kicked his cook until he dislocated his own toes. He believed that was the way to treat our natives.

Though he was a man of superior education and mentality, he did not realize that the Eskimos are independent and nothing can be accomplished with them by such methods.

He wanted to photograph the natives, and I agreed to

help him. One picture was to be of a mother with her child slung in her hood. The woman smilingly agreed to pose, but Dr. Wulff was dissatisfied with the appearance of her child and said: "Tell her that she's all right, but her baby is ugly as sin. Let her trade for the time being with that other woman there."

No mother in the world likes to hear it said that her child is not pretty enough to be photographed, so she refused to comply.

"Then I'll make her do it," he said, and tried to pull the squirming baby away from her. The woman bit and kicked, and all of her friends came to her aid. Dr. Wulff got no picture at all. He was so furious that I had to hold him to prevent his striking the women.

The dark season was rather dull, but in my house we were happier than ever. The boy developed nicely, and I had Dr. Wulff to entertain me with his stories of China and Japan, India and Bali.

Knud returned early in February, and Dr. Wulff and I planned to go south, visit Tasiussaq together and bring back Lauge Koch.

We decided to make the journey by dog sled via the icecap. I remember that it was on the big glacier that we saw the sun for the first time, about February 22nd. The Eskimos with us all removed their mittens and hoods, and asked us to do likewise. I complied, but Wulff laughed and said he had no intention of humoring the natives in such a stupid fashion, and kept on. Old Ulugatok from Cape York stopped him long enough to say:

"We are only poor, silly people who do as our fore-fathers have taught us to do. You should not laugh at us for this. We think that if we do this we shall not die at least until the sun returns next year. Even if it does no good, we enjoy life so much that we do anything to keep it."

We spent the night on the glacier and Dr. Wulff shivered all night. Next morning when we were ready to break camp he wanted to sleep a couple of hours longer. We thought it a strange mode of traveling, but waited for him. I intended to go straight along the glacier all the way to Cape York, but the natives were disgusted with Dr. Wulff and told me they were going to descend the glacier near Parker Snow Bay. I let them go, and Wulff and I drove on alone.

I was wary of the icecap and made a long detour to avoid the crevasses I knew were there; as a result we struck deep snow through which our progress was slow and difficult, but I knew that sooner or later we would be on smooth ice.

Soon I heard Wulff calling from behind me that he could go no further and we would have to make camp for the night. I laughed. We had been driving only four hours and that could scarcely be called a day's journey. But he said his heart was bad and, what was more, *he* was the man to decide how far we traveled each day.

I explained that this trip was merely a rehearsal to get him in condition for the trip to the north he had decided to make with Knud later on and that Knud certainly would make him finish a day's travel. However, we camped —I made a snow house—and slept a long time. Certainly he had enough rest—we had camped at two o'clock in the afternoon.

When we started out again we ran into terrible crevasses. At this point we should have turned down onto the ice along the shore, but I was sure we would soon be past the most dangerous ones, and we kept on. It was the worst route I had ever traveled. We passed crevasses more than thirty feet broad, and the snow bridges across the tops were frighteningly insecure.

Suddenly we heard one of the bridges crash behind us. The glacier was moving, and we were on top of it! I was panic-stricken, but dared not admit it to Wulff. Our only hope was to keep going. On all sides of us now were fresh, yawning crevasses. There was no turning back and no alternative but to try to reach the edge of the glacier and find a route to descend. I remember that I looked forward to the sea ice as I would have to paradise itself.

At that moment Dr. Wulff chose to lie down! No more for him today, he declared. His heart was troubling him and we would have to camp.

I scooped out a large hole in the ice, dumped our sleeping bags into it and we jumped in, pulling the sledges over the top. The wind made it difficult to cook, but we managed to brew some tea and soon felt better.

The snow came on the wind, drifting over us and filling up our hole. Dr. Wulff complained of the cold. It was like lying in a grave, he said. Yet there was nothing I could do. "Well," he grumbled, "I can't stay here. You'll have to get me out of this!"

That was impossible. He was furious and attempted to climb out of our hole—which would have been dangerous as we could not see two feet before our hands and he would surely have stumbled into a crevasse. I had to resort to force to keep him quiet, and he told me bitterly that I was a tyrant.

We lay there for two days, and when we finally climbed out most of the crevasses were hidden beneath a thin white layer of snow. After a while we were able to detect the crevasses by the slight depressions in the snow—an interesting phenomenon, but little help in our situation. We cooked some meat, and then set off in a dense fog.

Dr. Wulff crept along behind me. At one spot we had to cross a snow bridge which sagged six feet and hung across a gaping crevasse nearly forty feet wide. The bridge seemed thick, but I was timid and walked tremblingly out on it to test its strength. If I had fallen I dread to think what would have happened to Dr. Wulff, but there was nothing else to do. I held my breath and crossed, and then watched him come after me. Crevasse after crevasse we negotiated in that manner.

Again and again we detoured. Again and again we took our lives in our hands, but when the fog lifted we discovered that we had been traveling in a circle.

And then the doctor gave up. He was sullen, and said it was up to me to get us safely to Cape York.

We camped again. This was one trip I believed it would be impossible to complete. And as we lay sleeping we were wakened time after time by the roar of the glacier as it cracked and groaned and thundered its gargantuan body toward the sea.

After two more days of terror, we reached the edge of the glacier only to find it impossible to descend. The ice was jagged, cut in long, sheer slices like a crazily frosted wedding cake. Looking down we could see the smooth ice of the sea. And no way of reaching it!

We had to go back. I was horrified at the idea of re-tracing our steps. Wulff was hysterical and screamed that he would not do it, but I made him obey.

I was actually as frightened as he, but dared not let him know. We passed spots where the snow bridges had caved in; we even watched one huge mass of snow disappear and heard the thunder of it as it struck the earth hundreds of feet below.

Soon it grew dark and we had to stop. We were ex-hausted, our nerves raw, our sleeping bags wet. Our sup-ply of kerosene was low too, as Wulff had required warm tea in the middle of the day.

At last the moon rose, and I declared that we must keep going because it looked as if bad weather were coming and we should remain here no longer than was necessary.

Wulff stubbornly said that he would travel no farther. Poor man, he was actually ill from fear and discomfort, but I went on and he had to follow me. He kept yelling that he was tired, but I answered that I was as tired as he, and yet we must keep going if we were to save ourselves.

At last he dropped and began to unlash his load.

"You got me into this—now get me out!" he said an-grily. "You can't leave me here alone."

I protested once more, but he refused to move. "It is up to you to guide me when I'm ready to go. I'm tired now." Over and over he repeated this; I was growing anxious about his sanity.

At last in desperation I took my whip and cracked it in the air. He looked at me in bewilderment, and cried out that I dared not whip him. I said: "I not only dare, but it is my pleasure to do so, and I intend to do it immediately unless you get a move on."

"I'm not going to move until I have had some sleep," he shrieked.

I swung my whip in the white moonlight. To the right and to the left the lash crashed into the snow beside him. Closer and closer I let it crack, until he could feel it whiz past his ears. And then he jumped. He was terrified, and I realized that he was afraid of physical punishment; this gave me the upper hand. Never once did he try to defend himself, and a wave of sickness swept over me.

We came the rest of the way in silence. I knew that Wulff was suffering, but he said nothing; only his eyes pleaded with me to let him rest. Once in a while he cursed under his breath. That was what I wanted him to do—it was an indication of spirit. When we finally got out of the crevasses we lay down to rest. By the next morning, the atmosphere had changed. Wulff obeyed blindly without cursing and pleading for more sleep, and even volunteering to help harness the dogs.

"I can do more than I had believed myself capable of doing," he said, "and I thank you for forcing me to do it."

That gave him the victory over me—he had been frank with his appreciation. And I had believed him my enemy!

"But," he went on, "I can't go on to Cape York now. I really must go home and rest. This has been too much for me."

I agreed with him, and we turned to Thule after an absence of twenty days.

Knud was to leave shortly on his expedition with Dr.

Wulff to the north, and we decided that I had better stay at the post. I drove to Tasiussaq alone for a few supplies and to pick up Lauge Koch at the Nielsens', but I met him on the way—perhaps the Nielsens' daughter Jacobine had become too much of a problem for him.

I returned to Thule in time to see the mapping expedition off. Time after time while they were gone I thought of them fighting their way up there, and I wished I could have been with them. Yet what I was doing here was just as important and difficult.

Summer passed and fall arrived. It had been a bad year. The weather had prevented our hunting in kayaks, and ammunition was low.

Winter was at hand and the ice in—and still no word from Knud and his expedition. I planned to go north and cache meat along the route for them, but first I had to secure the meat. I tried to persuade some of the natives to accompany me north, but they excused themselves. It was the time when they had to remain beside the seals' blowholes to secure their own food. We went after the seals and managed to kill just enough to keep ourselves and our dogs alive.

But suddenly they ceased to show themselves. We hunted for blowholes and found them frozen over. There were no seals out in the open water, nor were there any walrus to be found.

Little Mequsaq was growing so lean that I was frightened. He still lived on his mother's milk, but she, too, was undernourished. Those were conditions in the fall of 1917.

In those times of stress I could not help admiring the tact of my wife. Each night when I returned from hunting

Navarana was at the beach waiting for me. Yet never did she ask if I had brought home any meat—she had merely come to help me with the dogs. But whenever I had a seal on the sledge she saw it immediately and shouted in surprise. She called anyone who happened to be in the house to come and admire her clever husband and his catch.

By the following fall, we still had no word of Knud. But one evening, we had a visitor—old Inaluk, the most gifted conjurer in Thule. While we were talking of Knud and his expedition, Inaluk suddenly left the house. A few moments later we heard her singing. We all ran out and saw her standing in the moonlight, her coat off, her long hair loosened and swinging as her body swayed from side to side:

"Those who have been on the Eastside are back.
Those who have been on the Eastside are back."

That was her song. When she finished singing, she said that Knud and his party were now coming home, "but two of them are missing."

"Is Knud missing?" I asked her.

She ceased her conjuring long enough to scoff: "Who suggests that the icecap and lack of food could bother Kunuk?"

After she had gone home, I lay reading in my bed. I could not get the woman's peculiar portent out of my mind, nor could I help feeling that there was evil in the air. Should I go up and look for them? I wondered. But where?

And then Knud's head poked through the door! I leaped

up with a shout to grasp his hand. I shall never forget that moment. The look of the icecap was upon him, months of starvation and hardship written on his face. It was several minutes before I inquired after the rest of the party.

"It has been a terrible summer," he said, "with such starvation and hardship as I have never known!"

"Are all of you here?" I asked.

"No. Two are missing," Knud answered.

He went into the kitchen to look for something to eat, and when he returned he said: "Henrik was eaten by the wolves, and Wulff fell by starvation. It is too horrible to think of."

We sat up all night, and Knud told me of his adventures. He laid out the whole trip before my eyes, and then wanted to know if I thought him in any way to blame for the misfortune. I told him then that I did not, and I still think so.

Dr. Wulff was dead. Unfit for such a journey, he had had neither the spirit of adventure to urge him onward nor the co-operation of the natives, all of whom disliked him. It must have been a terrible experience for him—the constant lack of food and the scarcity of game.

On the return home across the ice, Knud told me, they had no food but the dogs, and Wulff was sick and could not eat. When they had had to wade across the paralyzingly cold rivers on the icecap, he refused to follow, lying down and protesting that he would not take another step. Twice Knud had to recross the torrents to persuade him to come, and when at last they reached the land back of Etah he was completely exhausted.

Knud and Ajago had walked on ahead to Etah so that

Knud could find natives to return for the party and help them to safety. Knud had given orders to Wulff and Koch and the natives to remain at the spot where he had left them or, if they did go on, to follow a certain route. The natives were anxious to get home to their families, and they walked slowly on. Each time they climbed a hill they had to wait for Wulff who could not keep up with them. Once when they killed a rabbit he refused to eat any of the meat except the liver; he must have been very ill, mentally as well as physically. Then the cold began to affect him.

On several occasions Wulff had told Lauge Koch that he preferred going to his grave there on the icecap—he would not be sorry to be left behind as he had nothing to live for and there were few things in life he had not experienced. (He had made the same remark to me on our trip.) Still he lagged along, and insisted that he would only travel as fast as he chose.

I believe Lauge Koch's reckless honesty was the final blow to Wulff's ebbing vitality.

"How far do you estimate that we have gone today?" Wulff asked.

"About two and a half kilometers," Koch answered.

"How much farther must we go?"

"About seventy!"

That is not the best way to encourage a weary companion, but Koch believed this would frighten him and urge him to renewed efforts.

The natives killed two more rabbits, and these he also refused in spite of their liberal offers to give him any portions he preferred. Then he reiterated that he would go no further. Each time they stopped to rest it took hours to get him started again. Many times he told them to go on without him, but when they disappeared over a rise of ground he would call to them to wait, and this irked the natives. Lauge Koch stuck with Wulff, but it was difficult for him to placate the Eskimos.

Then finally, after a long rest, Wulff said:

"This is the end. I will not go any farther."

They heated a little water for him, and he lay down. They left him behind.

The natives told me later that they did not really believe Wulff was serious. He had been such a trial during the whole trip that they had thought him only lazy. Lauge Koch had exhausted his powers of persuasion and he, also, did not quite believe Wulff would fail to make another effort. He had done all it was humanly possible to do.

Lauge Koch was young and strong, and it would have been useless, and dangerous, for him to wait for Wulff to die. He had refused point-blank to go on and Koch's waiting would only have resulted in his own death as well.

The following day, I took some natives with me and started out for Etah where Koch was recuperating. On the way we looked for Dr. Wulff. He could not possibly have been alive, but I thought we might locate his body. We found the spot where Knud said they had left him, but he was not there.

I am positive that he regretted his decision to remain behind and tried to follow his companions, and lost his way.

And Henrik, one of the natives, was also dead. He had fallen asleep far from the others, while he was out after rabbits, and never returned. His companions looked for him only to discover three huge wolves instead, one of them smeared with blood.

When I arrived at Etah Lauge Koch was very weak, but after four days he was well enough to travel back to Thule.

We had had almost no meat during the whole summer and fall, and no walrus. By then it was December, and Knud asked us all to go out with him to look for walrus at Saunders Island. We knew there could be none at that time of year, but since Knud wanted to look we decided to humor him. When we got there we found that the ice had cracked up and the water, during the preceding night, had been covered with a new film of ice just strong enough to carry us and weak enough to permit the walrus to break through it to breathe. We got four big ones.

But the death of Dr. Wulff was always in our minds. We felt that there would always be some who would censure Lauge Koch for deserting him.

While we all knew the truth—there was nothing against him and, since he could not carry Wulff, it was his duty to save himself—we thought it might be better to see the action through in Greenland. There was an Inspector in Godhavn, and we felt it would be much simpler to have him settle the matter promptly than to see the tragedy dragged through the courts in Copenhagen.

We started for South Greenland, taking with us three Eskimos.

We decided to travel in separate divisions as it would be difficult to secure food for all of us if we went in one party. I drove with Lauge Koch and, of course, Navarana and Mequsaq, who was emerging into the great world for the first time.

We set out on a dark winter day, but made little speed because of the rough ice. The snow drifted badly and Navarana had to cover her hood entirely to protect the boy. Eventually, however, we reached a cave, built a fire and cooked some meat. The sheath of ice that lined the cavern flamed with a gemlike iridescence more brilliant than any man-made palace walls.

There was a sort of ledge which had been cut by previous travelers, and we had with us our large sleeping bag into which we crept with the boy between us.

Every family has its own problems. Ours was Mequsaq's habit of crawling up and playing instead of sleeping. To prevent this he was told that a great, ferocious bear walked up and down beside us during the night and looked for small boys who were not asleep. If the boys did not sleep they were likely to have their heads bitten off.

As we slept in the cave for some time while it continued to blow outside, the boy grew restless and crawled up to take a peek outside the bag. Imagine his consternation when he actually saw a bear standing close to him! The child hurried back into the sleeping bag with such alacrity that Navarana awakened and saw the bear standing beside us.

"Peter," she whispered hoarsely, "there is a big bear right in the cave with us."

There was no doubt about it—there *was* a bear. And he was between me and my gun. I yelled and jumped out of the bag, grabbing my pants from under the sleeping bag and stepping into them while I rose to my feet. In my nervousness I put both feet into one trouser leg. At the same moment I noticed that one of the natives was up and had his gun ready, but he could not shoot without endangering us, so I began to run. That is inconvenient with both one's feet in one leg of his trousers, and I toppled forward and rolled down the slope to the feet of the bear. He was as frightened as I was, and leaped away. The dogs had been attracted by the commotion, and a number of them tore loose from their traces and attacked the intruder. Itukusunguaq was now free to shoot and did so, but killed his best dog before he succeeded in getting the bear.

Mequsaq was thrilled by the performance and laughed loudly when he saw his father lying between the paws of the bear. Navarana brought him down to toss his little spear against the dead bear so that he might get his share. He had been the first to sight the animal, and she was as proud of him as if he had made the catch singlehanded.

We ran into one snowstorm before we reached Cape York, where we remained only one night. The natives had little meat of their own, so they could give us nothing.

That was one of the worst trips I have ever made. The weather vied with the ice to see which would get us. One day while the moon was obscured by clouds the rough ice broke my runners. It took so long to repair them that we were two days catching up with the party again. Fortunately there was enough snow to build igloos, but there was little meat to cook.

Finally our food supply came to an end. There was nothing for the dogs either, but we hoped soon to reach Cape Seddon which is on Melville Bay about halfway between Thule and Tasiussaq. We had friends there.

Lauge Koch now began to feel his weakness; his appetite was enormous, and his face looked haggard. We had nothing to give him except dog meat—one was killed each night. The gales toyed with us and made it almost impossible to keep going. I do not remember how many days we were out in the open, but it was so long that Navarana started to lose her milk. We fed the boy soup brewed from dog meat, but it did not agree with him—starving animals do not make very good soup—and we gave him a bone to chew on. Still he grew weaker and weaker, and I was afraid he would die. One evening he was too weak to nurse at all, and his poor mother sat as though petrified. There was nothing she could do for him. We took him between us in the sleeping bag, but we could scarcely keep warm ourselves. Lauge Koch's hunger burned from his eyes. His poor tortured body craved food, and he hammered the skulls of the starved, butchered dogs, to secure the brains. He even picked up the bones we had thrown away and gnawed them once more.

We finally reached Cape Seddon where the natives had meat and gave it to us willingly. Within a day all our travail was forgotten. The boy began to cry again—he had lain deathly quiet out on the ice—and once more there was milk and delicious food for him.

The trip from Cape Seddon to Tasiussaq was easy.

When we arrived at Tasiussaq, Knud said, "It would be nice for Navarana to have her baby down here and get it over before going home."

That was how I first learned of the advent of another child. In the evening I asked Navarana if this was true,

Knud with Mequsaq.

and she admitted it was. "Why did you tell Knud before you told me?"

"Because he is going to Denmark and won't hear about it there. But you have enough to worry about now, so I thought I should wait."

That night she danced and enjoyed herself for many hours, as she did for several nights following.

We continued south from Tasiussaq in small divisions. At Pröven Little Jonas had to dig down in his caches to provide food for us. He did not actually object, but he could not resist hinting of times to come when provisions might not be so plentiful. Perhaps Kaiser Wilhelm would send up his submarines; Little Jonas' place at Pröven was, he said, an especially strategic point. If the Germans captured it they could control the whole catch of white whales and get all the *mattak* they wanted. He had prepared to go inland in such an emergency, and had transported big caches there. Knud made him go for the meat. Little Jonas sighed—but who could resist Knud?

The inspector at Godhavn said that he was willing to hold the court we sought. But now Lauge Koch refused to submit to such a trial. He had visited the scientific station on Disko Island and the Danes there had advised him against it. What arguments they used on him I never knew; whatever they said I am sure they meant to be for his best interests.

From Godhavn, where Koch had left our party, we went to Ritenbenk where Administrator Andersen, the best host in Greenland, lived. We arrived the Saturday before Easter, only to find that he was on a trip to Umanak Colony to invite guests for Easter. His maid, Old Sofie, a famous cook and the devoted caretaker of his property, was none too pleased to see us. "We" were fairly numerous at the moment, as Knud had invited everyone along the road to accompany us.

On the wall outside the house hung an entire caribou and two hindquarters—the reason for the invitations Andersen was issuing. First we took down the hindquarters and forced poor Old Sofie to cook steaks. She was a fine cook even when made to perform against her will. When that was done she refused to remain in the house, and walked out in protest. We then took down the whole caribou and finished that as well. Knud then went down into the cellar.

"He has wine," Knud shouted, "wine in wartime!" I must admit that he had no wine when we left.

We later heard that Administrator Andersen had spent his Easter eating hardtack and barley soup. Sofie had complained of our violence, but Mr. Andersen thought it a wonderful joke and regretted that he himself had never done likewise.

We went on to Jakobshavn, where our trip culminated. The celebration there, in honor of our coming, is still remembered in Greenland. First a coffee party was given for all the natives. Then a dance, and another, and finally until everyone but Knud was exhausted. At Jakobshavn, we said goodbye to Knud; he sailed for Denmark and we started back north to Thule.

On the way, Navarana became ill. I was unable to diagnose the trouble, but I could see that she was in a critical condition, burning with fever. When we got to Tasiussaq, the doctor there said it was pneumonia—and the baby might be born at any moment.

That same afternoon a little girl was born.

Navarana wanted to get up next day and travel, but the doctor advised against it, and we decided she should not go north until fall, and that in the meantime she should stay with the Nielsens.

I, of course, had to get back north immediately in time for the hunting season and left Tasiussaq a few days after the birth of the baby, whom we had named Pipaluk.

Spring was half gone by the time I reached Melville Bay.

I decided to save time by hunting at Cape York instead of going all the way to Thule until time for the birds at Saunders Island.

The spring passed and summer came without the arrival of a ship. Hunting can be monotonous, and it was now. There was no kerosene and no ammunition, so I had to resort to harpoons. But the sun did not go below the horizon for four months, so I could not complain.

I dreamed constantly of Navarana and the two youngsters, but I had to stay where there was game, and during the whole summer there was no way of my seeing them.

In the fall I went south for my family. Melville Bay! How many times have I traversed it! But how much easier it seemed when I knew I would find my wife and children at the other end of it.

At Tasiussaq I found Navarana, Mequsaq and Pipaluk in the bloom of health. Pipaluk looked much more like a

Top: Harpooning a seal.
Bottom: Hauling a walrus out of the water.

white child than did her husky brother. He had learned to talk a little, and was full of the devil.

My arrival and reunion with my family was the occasion of a celebration for the natives. A few days later it was discovered that Mequsaq had worn out his first pair of soles—another celebration! And there was still a third before we left.

We took the trip back to Thule slowly as the children had to become accustomed to native foods after the fine bread and delicacies they had eaten at the Nielsens'.

When we reached Thule, life was normal again. Navarana had grown up now in every way. The mother of two children, a woman of experience and travel, she could not now be looked down upon by anyone.

Not long after we had gotten back home, wolves suddenly appeared in Thule. Formerly there had been almost none, but when the men of the community went to Ellesmere Land to hunt, the wolves followed them back in the sledge tracks. It was terrible to see them prowling on the hills looking down at the children playing about our houses.

I had caught two bear cubs that fall and they made fine pets for the children for a while. Every morning the two cubs stood outside and waited until sounds of life within assured them that Mequsaq and Pipaluk were awake, then they stalked in silently. Next came my old king dog, Ersulik. He was old and worn out, reduced to little more than a plaything. Then there were always at least two pups. The old dog was tortured unmercifully. Mequsaq and his friends played hunting games, and Ersulik was always the prey. They attached chairs and boxes to his tail and made

him haul them about the floor. One day I heard him yip
and ran to discover the trouble. Mequsaq had run a fork
into his left eye. The poor dog was blind in that eye forever after, but his love for the boy never faltered.

The bears were good wrestlers, but eventually they grew
too big and strong. The children cried once, and said that
the bears had beaten them in their games. I chained the
cubs outside, but the children still continued to play with
them, so I had to put them in a cage after that.

The spring came and I was happy. Navarana was a bit
huskier and looking her best in anticipation of the great
event of her life—a trip to Denmark to see the white people in their own country and learn many things from them.
This she had been anticipating for years, and now that the
voyage was imminent she spent all her time making ele-
gant clothes for herself and the children.

We had talked it over and come to the conclusion that
this was the best time to make the trip. We would go down
to Tasiussaq by sledge and catch a boat there. We might
never get through to Denmark as we had had no recent
news of the war, but the latest gossip we had heard seemed
to indicate that Germany was about to give up.

I went to fetch some dog food for the trip. We would not
need much as the seals were abundant on the ice, but it
would be well to have something in reserve for the children
in case of bad weather.

Mequsaq was only three at the time. He saw me setting
out and, joined by a little boy his own age, toddled after
me. I did not notice them. When I returned home it was
to discover that they were nowhere about so I hurried out
to look for them. There they were, two small dots wad-

dling across the ice, playing as they went and unaware of the lurking danger which tracked them—two gaunt wolves.

I shall never forget how fast I ran, faster than I ever dreamed I could, yet I was too far away to head off the wolves. I knew too that I should not shout: I had been told that when a wolf is disturbed he will sometimes jump on his prey in a last desperate effort to capture it. The wolves were almost abreast of the children when in my desperation I called upon luck, aimed my gun and pulled the trigger. Luck was with me; I hit one of the animals in the spine. The other heard the report of the gun and bolted.

The two little boys were not in the least surprised or frightened at what had happened. The sound of the shot was to them the most natural thing in the world. By the time I reached them they were sitting beside the dead animal playing with it.

With our sledge filled with enough provisions to carry us across Melville Bay we left Thule. Two other families accompanied us south to trade. The little auks were already chattering in the cliffs, and the fine ice in Melville Bay permitted us to make haste.

We arrived at Tasiussaq in record time and remained there until the water opened up.

Finally, after weeks of waiting and exhausting our meager fund of gossip concerning the war, a ship steamed into the harbor.

On board was Mr. Daugaard-Jensen, president of the Royal Greenland Trading Company which managed all the trading posts colonized in Greenland. He was a most pleasant and agreeable man with a heart big enough to accommodate everyone in Greenland, but naturally he was none too pleased with me. Knud and I were the only two traders in all Greenland outside the supervision of the Royal Company. The organization had not bothered with Thule, thinking that nobody would be fool enough to try to establish a post there.

As this was the first steamship to visit Greenland since the war, space was at a premium, and there was no room for us. Perhaps, we were told, if we waited, we could get space on the *Thorvaldsen*, one of the last two sailing vessels plying between Denmark and Greenland, which was scheduled to call.

11

The *Thorvaldsen* arrived at last—a fine vessel commanded by Captain Hansen. We had a little trouble persuading him to take the bears along, but I finally told him that they were gifts for the King from the natives, and that made everything all right.

The trip was uneventful but pleasant, for me at least. Navarana thought it was monotonous, especially as our fresh water was limited, and she could not accustom herself to washing her face in the brine.

We encountered a little difficulty when we reached the mine-laden waters of the North Sea. A patrol boat approached us and warned us of danger, but this was only after we were deep within the danger zone, and it would have been quite as dangerous for us to turn back as to proceed. To maneuver a heavily laden sailing vessel through narrow lanes dotted with mines is something of a trick, and Captain Hansen issued orders for the passengers to sleep fully clothed. He set a course and held to it, and on the 11th of December, 1918, we sailed safely into the harbor of Copenhagen and the bustle of newspapermen and parents and relatives which one anticipates for so long and so soon wishes to be rid of By the end of the first evening I was all for turning around and returning to Greenland.

Navarana, like all Eskimos visiting civilization for the first time, was disappointed. White men are apt to exaggerate the commonplaces of their homeland.

"Oh, I thought the houses were bigger," she said. "They are not much higher than an iceberg."

Only two things impressed her: first, it was winter and the sun was shining; second, she noticed a team of horses eating from their nose bags while being driven about— Navarana considered this device certain proof of white men's intelligence.

Next day we had an audience with the King. The ruler of our country was gracious and asked Navarana what she thought of Denmark.

Navarana turned to me: "Is that man really the King we have heard so much about? How can he think for everybody in Denmark if he is stupid enough to suppose I have any opinions about this magnificent land after only one day's stay?"

"What does she say?" asked the King.

I translated freely: "Your Majesty, she thinks it is wonderful and grand!"

"I thought so!" said the King, and was content.

Afterwards we went to my father's home where she stayed with the children. I had accepted several invitations to lecture and could not be with her as much or as often as I wished. She grew tired, I am sure, of sitting about doing nothing, and would have preferred being in a house of her own where she could cook what she wanted and say what she thought. She had everything she needed, she said, but all things came too easily. She had no feeling of living when there were no difficulties to surmount.

An epidemic of Spanish influenza swept over Europe, and I contracted it. I was walking along the streets of Copenhagen one day when suddenly I felt dizzy. I staggered up to a couple of policemen and asked them to call me a taxi. Unfortunately there was a telephone strike on at the moment, and they could not call for a cab. Also, they thought I was drunk. When I denied this it only convinced them they had been right and they bundled me off to the police station where, fortunately, I was recognized and rushed to a hospital.

I was kept there for four months, and for a long time was so ill that I was isolated in a ward reserved for dying patients. I remember that the room was meant to accommodate six beds, but the epidemic raged so furiously that one morning eleven patients were brought in alive and nine bodies carried away before evening. I was one of the lucky ones who survived.

I was so weak after being released from the hospital that I could not walk for a long while. My hair fell out. I was thinner than I had ever been, and tortured with sciatica. It looked as though I would be incapacitated for months. When Knud came to visit me, he said that he had talked with the doctor and had decided to send another man up to Thule to replace me for a while. I protested, but when Mr. Nyboe also agreed with Knud and the doctor, I had to submit to their judgment.

This was my first serious defeat, and it was a great blow to me.

I went to a little island, Slotoe, to rest for a few weeks, and when I got back to Copenhagen I spent some time with Knud. He was planning an expedition for the following year into Hudson Bay to study the Eskimos there and was counting on both me and Navarana to help. He suggested that Navarana return to Thule as soon as possible and supervise the sewing of clothes for the expedition, then come back down to Tasiussaq during the late winter where we would join her the following summer.

We discussed this with Navarana and she was anxious to do it for, while she liked Copenhagen, she was tired of being a curiosity. The citizens had been tactless, staring at her as she passed on the streets, offering her money and fingering her garments. She would be glad to get back to Greenland.

We decided to leave Pipaluk with my parents. Both my father and mother were anxious to keep her, and Navarana said she wanted the little girl to have the advantages of Denmark—and the safety.

While I had been in Denmark Knud and I had had built a ship of our own, the *Soekongen,* a sturdy little boat constructed especially for ice navigation and expeditions. Its cost had been almost prohibitive, but we found that, after the war, the prices of our furs skyrocketed and we had much more cash on hand than we had anticipated. Captain Pedersen was commanding our boat.

It was arranged that Navarana and Mequsaq would sail for Greenland on the *Soekongen,* which they did a few days later, while I went back to the island of Slotoe to complete my recuperation.

But a telegram from Knud changed everything. He had received word from Captain Pedersen that he had run into a gale, broken his bowsprit, and had had to stop in at Norway to have it repaired. A short time later, between Norway and Scotland, he had lost the boom and had to dock in Scotland where he had lost more valuable days. Chances were he and Navarana would not reach Tasiussaq until fall, and we would have to arrange to take them from there to Thule by sledge during the winter.

At this same time, Knud's long telegram went on, Lauge Koch was going north with an expedition of his own and planned to operate in the Thule District. As his ship was small, he had asked if we could arrange to transport a portion of his supplies.

Both Knud and I were needed; there was no doubt of that. A steamer was sailing the next day for Upernavik—the last boat of the year. Could I go along? the telegram asked.

By a miracle, I was on that steamer with Knud the following day. When we landed at Upernavik, we were told that the ice to the north was worse than usual. A few days later Lauge Koch appeared with his schooner, which had been furnished by the Danish government, and I accompanied him as pilot northward across Melville Bay while Knud remained to await our ship. The boat was overloaded, and goods were piled high on deck. Koch had brought dog food—dried fish—from South Greenland and piled it on top of everything else. In fact, to reach the deckhouses one had to burrow through holes.

He had more food than was ever seen before with a Danish expedition. Koch had accepted an offer from the government to help him outfit the expedition—hence, the

Pipaluk and myself just before I left Denmark
for the Hudson Bay expedition.

unbelievable amount of food, so much that we had trouble in devouring our daily rations.

I was a very poor helper. My weakness and sciatica made it painful even to stand at the wheel.

A gale blew up and the ice began to pack around us. During the storm I fell in the water and soaked my clothes. When we had gotten through the worst ice, the snow began falling steadily, and I had to remain in the crow's-nest for twenty-four hours in my wet garments.

When the sun returned, my sciatica was cured. Everything the doctor had told me to avoid as a death penalty, I had disregarded. Since that time I have never felt a twinge in the nerves of my leg.

We reached Thule and were about to set out for Lauge Koch's northern destination when we heard the natives yelling. They were announcing another ship—the *Soekongen*—with Knud, Navarana and Mequsaq aboard.

Seldom had I seen Navarana so happy. She danced with joy to be at home once more—she could not put into words the emotions she felt.

Knud and I sailed north next day with Lauge Koch and his provisions. It was an enormous job unloading his supplies, which included two tractors, and we had barely finished the work when a gale broke out. We sailed off, leaving Koch to his own fate. We felt, however, that we need waste no sympathy on him. He was a fine young man, quite capable of accomplishing whatever he set out to do.

At Thule we said good-bye once more to Navarana and the boy. Navarana was to supervise the making of clothing for the expedition, and she had arranged for the boy to be taken care of by a missionary when she left Thule to join us for the Hudson Bay expedition.

Knud boarded a navy ship at Egedesminde that would take him back to Denmark to complete the preparations, while I sailed with Captain Pedersen and the *Soekongen* to the southernmost part of Greenland to investigate the old Viking ruins there. The plan was for me to go back to Denmark to fulfill some lecture commitments after investigating the Viking ruins.

It was Christmastime when I reached Copenhagen again, and I spent the holiday with my parents, my brothers and sisters and little Pipaluk, who had turned into a lovely little girl and was accustomed to all the comforts and privileges she had never known before.

In addition to lecturing, I was busy assisting Knud with the details of the Hudson Bay expedition. Captain Pedersen was to transport us from Greenland to Hudson Bay, and he was a man always to be trusted. Two young scientists, Dr. Birket-Smith and Dr. Therkel Mathiassen, were to accompany us as ethnologists, and as an assistant we were to have the young writer, Helge Bangsted.

A chance to combine anthropological research with money-making arose in the person of Schnedler-Sorensen, a Danish film producer who offered us the capital to film a travel and adventure motion picture. It was decided that I should leave for Greenland ahead of the main party, with Schnedler-Sorensen and an actor to film the movie which we had often planned to make.

And so in May, I set out once more for Greenland, this time as a motion picture director. We shot a few scenes on the voyage and more at Ivigtut. From there we sailed to

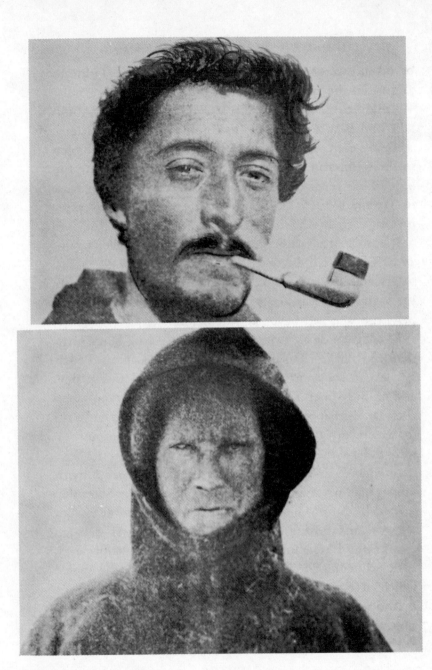

Top: Helge Bangsted.
Bottom: Dr. Therkel Mathiassen.

Julianehaab, at the extreme southern tip of Greenland, on an oil tanker and I arranged a big dance in which I took part and grouped the entire colony in the background. We photographed everything, including the Eskimo cattle farmers, leaving not the least thing of interest unrecorded before we returned to Ivigtut.

That year was 1921, the two hundredth anniversary of the arrival in Greenland of Hans Egede, the "Apostle of Greenland," who first brought Christianity to the pagan Eskimos. A great celebration was planned, and the King of Denmark had consented to dignify the event by his presence. As it was the first time any king had ever visited Greenland, everyone was in a state of wild excitement. The principal celebration was to be held at Godthaab, the settlement founded by Hans Egede, and every person who could get there planned to attend.

I arrived in Godthaab on a Saturday, the day before the opening of the week-long celebration. Sunday was to be devoted to prayer and thanksgiving. The town was crowded with two bishops and an assortment of high priests, ministers and simple teachers of the gospel.

Knud Rasmussen and his wife were there too. She had come up with Knud on the *Soekongen* to bid him good-bye when we sailed for Hudson Bay.

At 9:30 Sunday morning I received a message from the Supreme Bishop of Denmark informing me that he had mistakenly failed to invite me to take part in the procession at ten o'clock. Would I be there?

I had had only three hours' sleep, but I leaped out of bed and made for the line of march. The procession was already under way, marching slowly and seriously, chanting

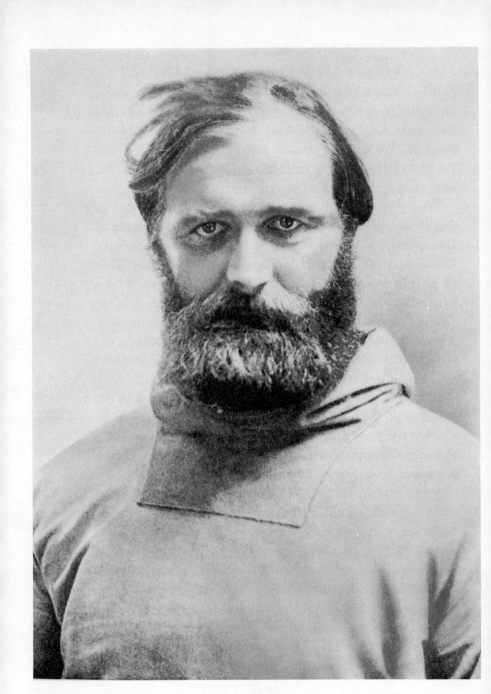

*Myself in 1921, photographed in Godthaab
at the only Eskimo studio in the world.*

as it traversed the distance between the school and the church. I hid behind a house and waited until the first dignitaries had passed by. Then I saw the native editor of the Greenlander paper in the ranks, and I thought that would be about my place, so I joined him. We continued to walk slowly and solemnly.

Later I was somewhat shocked to learn that the one and only discordant note in the whole procession was my blouse, which was made of scarlet cloth originally intended for a pillow slip. The bishops and high priests apparently could not appreciate the variation of color. I thought it relieved the monotony; they thought it disgraceful.

But at the moment I was innocent of the stir I caused. As reverent as anyone, I walked into the church where I sat down, pleased with my own piety, and awaited the blessing. After the ceremony was over I proceeded to the school for coffee and pious conversation.

On the next following Saturday the King arrived in the harbor. This event had been anticipated as the high point in the week of festivities. His Majesty disembarked with his whole family and was greeted at the pier by every notable of Greenland. (The authorities had made certain about a uniformity of costume this time, and white blouses were *de rigueur*. I behaved myself and was a model of servility.)

It was a great day for the natives. The King had promised to dispense coffee, which everyone expected to be extraordinary. When the drink turned out to be merely plain coffee, the natives were sullen with disappointment. He could not have known that the bishops had stolen his thunder the previous Sunday by feeding the entire population coffee and cookies, figs, dried prunes and cigars.

Next day there was a big banquet aboard the King's yacht. All the prominent Danes and natives were invited to attend, and the royal family graciously mingled with the throng. After a suitable interval the King went below and remained there. His adjutant walked through the crowd with a long paper on which were written numerous names, and spoke to those whose names appeared on the list. One by one they entered the cabin from the starboard side. Shortly each one emerged from the port side knighted or with a medal or order of some sort pinned to his chest. Those of us who had not yet been approached by the officer stood about in nervous groups chatting desperately about the weather, our eyes following the King's adjutant.

Presently the King reappeared on the bridge. Those faces that did not beam over a cross or a medal were darkly brooding. Their hopes were shattered.

"Peter Freuchen, I want to talk to you!" shouted the King. I jumped toward my sovereign—everyone witnessed my triumph.

"I want to give you something I know you will appreciate," said the King. "Please come below."

I followed him down the stairs.

The King picked up a large bottle containing a live beech branch, a branch he had cut himself the day before he left home. (The beech is the national tree of Denmark, and the King's love for it is well known.) He explained to me that each day on the journey he had nurtured it with fresh water and cut an inch from the branch, hammering the new end to keep the leaves fresh.

"And now," he said, "I shall give you one of the leaves!"

I stood for a moment holding the beech leaf, and feeling somewhat ridiculous.

The royal buffet pleased the natives immensely. The King and Queen themselves served the guests. I saw the King pick up a large cake and present it to one of the natives. "Very good," said the dignified Eskimo. "This is the way one expects a king to serve his guests!" He took the whole cake from the King and proceeded to eat it. The party was a great success, and the tables were stripped clean before they were abandoned.

Soon afterward the King's ship steamed out of the harbor and the colony slowly settled back into its usual routine.

Shortly after the King's departure, Knud and I left for Thule on the *Soekongen*. Mrs. Rasmussen had already sailed for Denmark. We stopped at Jakobshavn to secure dog food and other necessities for the Hudson Bay expedition. There we learned the most exciting news that had come to us for a long time in the Arctic.

A large Danish passenger ship, the *Bele,* had run upon the rocks during a dense fog. The King's vessel had picked up the SOS and, changing course, proceeded to the rescue of the eighty-three passengers and members of the crew of the *Bele.* The King's boat had also been hampered by the fog, and had nosed about trying to avoid the same rocks which the *Bele* had struck. But after three days the fog lifted and the King sighted the wreck.

Without a moment's hesitation he hurried to the wreck in a little motorboat. Most of the survivors were cast up on a desolate island and protected from the elements by tents made of sails and tarpaulin.

197

When the captain of the *Bele* saw his king coming to save him he burst into tears, and cried:

"You are not only a king, but you are also a *man!*"

That simple expression was perhaps the best, and sincerest, compliment ever paid to the then King of Denmark.

We had planned to supply our post at Thule with enough goods to last a year, and most of those provisions had been on the *Bele*. We were at a loss to know what to do, so we sailed to Tasiussaq.

Navarana was already there. She had traveled down from Thule on a sledge and had all the clothes ready for the expedition, but she was not very well. She had fallen victim to a cold germ and was in very poor health.

She came on board the *Soekongen,* and we decided to sail to the *Bele* to salvage whatever we could.

When we got there, we saw that the wreck was doomed, but because the inspector of North Greenland realized that the hulk might be washed away at any moment, he permitted us to break up the deck and try to recover our goods.

When we had secured everything possible out of the *Bele,* we sailed to Upernavik, where we were joined by Dr. Mathiassen and Dr. Birket-Smith, who had come up to Greenland on the *Bele*.

Navarana was still very ill. It was difficult for her to walk, and we carried her from the harbor to the house of the post manager, where I remained with her while Knud and his party went on to Thule.

It was apparent by now that she had Spanish influenza, the same disease to which I had fallen victim the year before. I did not leave her side, and though she was thankful that I could be with her, she was torn with anxiety for her children. She would have liked me to go up to Thule and see that Mequsaq was being cared for properly.

The next day Navarana was worse. The doctor was off on a trip at the time, and there was nothing we could do for her. In the evening she asked me what I thought was the matter. Her head was buzzing with thoughts which came unsummoned, she said. It was ghastly to sit helpless and watch her fade away. I told her to try to sleep, but she could not.

After a while she began to talk about her visit to Denmark and the things she had seen there. That had been the high point in her life.

Then she took my hand in hers and told me how happy she had been in having a husband who would talk with her as an equal. And finally she said that she was very sleepy.

I went into the kitchen to brew tea for her. As I sat and waited for the water to boil, it came over me how much I loved her and how much she had developed since our marriage.

Navarana was so quiet that I tiptoed in to look at her. As I watched, her lip just quivered. Then she was dead.

I refused to believe it. My dear little wife was dead. I sat petrified. For the first time in my life I was in the presence of the death of someone close to me. My past life had been happy and carefree, and suddenly I found myself the father of two motherless children.

During the making of arrangements for the coffin and funeral, I was almost unconscious of anything that happened, and had lost interest in everything. But soon something happened which brought me to life with a vengeance.

The minister in Upernavik came to me with the statement that, since Navarana had died a pagan, she could not be buried in the graveyard. No bell might toll over her funeral and, he was sorry, he could not deliver a sermon.

It was relaxing for me to be so furious. I told him to go to the devil with his bells and his sermons, but my wife would sleep in the cemetery and not be thrown to the dogs. Still, he said, he had already warned his congregation of the horrible consequences of dying without baptism, and this was his opportunity to offer them an example.

I am glad that I did not strike him. I had the good grace only to tell him to get out and let me manage the service.

It was the most pitiful funeral I have ever witnessed. The workers of the colony acted as pallbearers. I remember that I was angry at the blacksmith because he smoked a cigar during the procession.

Hidden behind the rocks and houses were the natives, terrified at the approach of this funeral procession which had not been solemnized by a minister nor sanctioned by the tolling of bells from the church. They dared not follow such a pagan to her final resting place, my little Navarana who had fed and entertained them whenever they visited her.

These were the sad tidings I had to relate to Knud when he returned from Thule. He had adored Navarana. She made her own memorial in the clothes she had put together for our expedition. We had always counted upon her for so many things. The two of us climbed up to her grave and said good-bye for the last time and sailed away to new chapters in our lives.

12

I tried to drown my grief in furious activity, completing the preparations for our departure on the Hudson Bay expedition.

Knud had brought three families of Eskimos down from Thule to be our helpers on the Hudson Bay expedition. They were all curious about their Canadian cousins, and were fine men and women, but they fell sick, probably infected by the same germs which had slain Navarana.

Added to this, our small ship was overcrowded when we left Upernavik and we had not even picked up the full load awaiting us in Godthaab.

At any rate, we were already cramped with scientists and natives lying three men to a bunk, which gave each man eight hours' sleep if he held to a fixed schedule. We also had about seventy dogs, and these had to be watched constantly to keep them from fighting.

Our motion picture cameraman had been to Thule and secured all the pictures he needed for the travel and scenic film, and he left us at Godthaab to return to Denmark. The director and the actor had gone long since, the director unable to endure what he termed "the hardships."

At Godthaab the poor natives grew worse, and the doc-

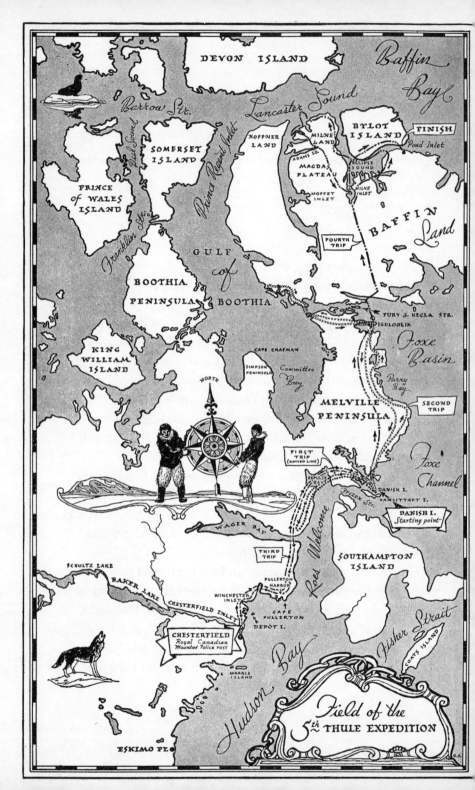

tor gave up hope for Iggianguaq, our best hunter. His wife sat beside him and held his hand, crying as she stroked his head.

When Knud asked the other natives who were to accompany us on the expedition if they wouldn't rather turn back in view of the unlucky start, the oldest of the Eskimos, who all lay sick, raised himself in his bed and said:

"We have been saying that we have only one fear, and that is that we might not get well in time to go along."

And so, in 1921, we sailed out of Godthaab with Captain Pedersen at the wheel on the greatest expedition of all, the largest one led by Knud Rasmussen, on which he visited and studied all the existing Eskimo tribes in Canada.

The natives began to recover almost as soon as we sailed. Our course took us across Davis Strait to Baffin Land to Hudson Strait where we tried to make connection with natives as we ran up north of Savage Islands; however, we saw none and had little time to waste looking for them. The season was late, and we knew we would have plenty of ice to fight in the bay as it was. We had to anchor in Gordon Bay to await the lifting of heavy fog. While we lay there I saw more seals collected in one place than I have ever seen anywhere else. They popped up around the ship like minnows in a pond; what they fed upon I do not know.

The fog persisted, and we could see almost nothing of the country. A Hudson's Bay Company post was supposed to be situated in Gordon Bay, but we had no map to locate it—the map had gone down with the *Bele*.

Finally we sailed out of the western end of Hudson

Top: *Knud and Dr. Birket-Smith.*
Bottom: *A Cape York native who was along
on the Hudson Bay expedition.*

Strait, setting a course to the north of Southampton Island, and thence heading straight for Lyon Inlet where we planned to make our headquarters on Winter Island, the place where Parry had stopped a hundred years earlier. He had come up from the south and, minus a propeller, had been caught there by the ice. We believed that we would have better luck and could drive north and south with our dogs, seeking out the natives. No one who knew the Eskimo tongue had ever talked with them before.

But we, too, ran into bad ice. The ice one finds around Greenland, on both east and west coasts, is treacherous and never to be relied upon. It grips the traveler, holds him, carries him about and smashes him. It is ever on the move, ever changing. But here in Hudson Bay we encountered for the first time in our lives ice that froze and remained where it froze, some of it gray and rotten and lifeless.

We made very slow progress. Resorting to all the tricks we knew, we accomplished only a few miles a day through the jungle of ice. It was also difficult to ascertain our direction, for the clouds blanketed the sun and our compasses were entirely useless so close to the Magnetic North Pole.

The wind howled and the days on board became increasingly wretched. It was only Captain Pedersen's fine humor and his way of keeping up the morale of the crew that saved our senses. "To hell with it," he would cry, "we can't stay here all winter, so let's keep going west. There's got to be land there."

And then one day sure enough there was land ahead—a low range of mountains materialized through the fog. I did not know where we were, nor did anyone else, but as we approached it looked like Winter Island as described in

Parry's book, and the fjord had the appearance of Lyon Inlet.

There was still no sun and we discovered no harbor in the island, and so we sailed on toward the mainland, where soon we discovered what would serve as a harbor. Explorers who have been at sea for a long while and who realize that the water will freeze shortly and lock the boat in for the winter are modest in their demands for a harbor. We also discovered a small lake, saw a few rabbits on the hill, and a handy location for setting up a house. We were satisfied.

Knud's motorboat was lowered into the water and the dogs hurried to land. They were so filthy and so lean that they scarcely looked like dogs. They made a bee line for the pond and drank till their bellies bulged. Not until then did they stop to sniff and explore the place on legs stiff from long disuse.

Captain Pedersen had promised to remain, if possible, and help us set up our house. Finally everything was unloaded and we bade him farewell. He was not sure that he could make his way out through the ice, which was now freezing solid, but his face betrayed no anxiety—it never has in his life. We could see the boat fighting valiantly along for five days. On the sixth morning it was gone from sight, and we settled down to our own problems.

We shared the work as usual. Knud took the natives with him and set out to determine the location of the land we occupied and also to secure meat for ourselves and the dogs. He was always lucky and I never was; therefore, I remained at home and finished our house, which still lacked a roof. According to the map we were building a

Top: *Captain Peder Pedersen, Knud and myself.*
Bottom: *"The Bellows."*

house on the open sea. We knew, however, that there was earth under us, and that the map must be wrong.

We called our house "The Bellows." It was of modest appearance and crowded to live in. But we all had high spirits and the will to work. Fourteen persons lived in that little house; at first we thought it was a bit uncomfortable and crowded, but Knud was a man who could always put up "one more."

Knud returned finally with news and provisions. He had discovered that we were situated on a tiny island, and the mainland near us supported herds of caribou. He had shot twelve and a number of seals. There were also many walrus in the sea outside, so we were assured that we would not starve. That was the important thing, and it gave us confidence in the success of our expedition.

None of us had seen any native Eskimos, but a few old stone caches made us certain that we would find them eventually. At any rate, it was nice to be free of them until everything was in order. The worst part of it was that the wind roared, and the snow drifted ceaselessly. The house was warm but terribly crowded. Since our plan was to remain in the field most of the time, however, we did not complain of this.

Eventually we discovered that the island we occupied was a bit of unmapped territory and that the piece of land Knud had thought to be the mainland was in reality Vansittart Island. We were much farther from any habitation than we had thought.

As soon as the ice was hard Knud and I left to discover the native Eskimos—if any lived about. We traveled up the fjord and came to a narrow sound through which ran a swift current. It was, we later learned, Hurd Channel, which never freezes.

Traveling along an unknown coast, not knowing what or whom to expect next, is the most exciting experience in the world. We intended to go as far as Repulse Bay in our search. When we left Greenland it was not known whether or not there was any trading post north of Fullerton Harbor, so we followed the ice on the west side of Hurd Channel to make our way out to Frozen Strait and on up to the Hudson's Bay Company station at Repulse.

Soon we discovered a sledge standing not far from a cache containing half a bearded seal. The sledge was a clumsy affair, badly constructed, and the seal was left in the cache without being cut up. Whoever had left it had merely sliced it in two, and placed no stones beneath it to prevent its freezing fast to the ground. Our Greenland Eskimos would never have left meat in that condition.

As we advanced farther along we began to recognize the coast from Parry's description and, as it was unwise to come upon strange people after dark, we made camp.

The next day we set out again as soon as it was light and before long we came upon the tracks of a sledge. From the tracks we could see that the sledge itself was very narrow, the runners broad. Far in the distance were black dots moving through the snow.

We urged our dogs to their greatest speed in order to arrive among the natives in an impressive manner. The Eskimos stopped when they saw us coming and grabbed their guns. I was a little frightened, and shouted to Knud. He yelled back that he would go ahead and meet them first.

He took off his mittens and raised his bare hands in the air. We followed his example. Instantly the natives dropped their weapons and stuck up their hands. We halted our dogs and stood quiet a few moments to give them time to look us over.

After a little while the chief stepped forward and said: "We are only plain, common people."

"We also are only plain, common people," said Knud.

They had thought, because of our white clothes and sledges, that we were ghosts, and our whips had frightened them still more. This was the first step toward a friendship of four years' duration between the natives and ourselves. The chief's name was Pappi (The Birdtail) and the three families with him belonged to the Netchilik tribe.

It was no great treat to visit this tribe, for they had no food whatever. We brought in some oatmeal from our supply, and one of the women, whose body was tattooed all over, simply dumped it in her pot of old soup. The mixture was terrible to the taste. I noticed that she herself ate nothing, but she later explained to me that she was pregnant, and therefore not permitted to eat from the same pot as the rest of us.

Their dogs were shabby runts and could hardly keep up with ours next day when we left for Repulse Bay together.

Knud was already their dearest friend, and wormed every secret out of them. He soon knew that in this country three different tribes of natives lived near each other, yet kept apart socially. Each tribe considered the other two vastly inferior.

By the time he had been in this region two days, he spoke the dialect of all the tribes and we got to know them, although they were not accustomed to having white men come and go as though they belonged to the tribe.

Knud got them to tell and reveal things that no one had ever known. Their entire mystical, spiritual life is clearly brought out in the books he wrote following this expedition. To a lot of people an Eskimo is an Eskimo. That's entirely wrong. They are all different. These isolated people, who wander around alone day and night, gave birth to remarkable thoughts and develop along many different lines.

In no time at all everybody in the vicinity of Repulse Bay knew that we were coming. One after another, we heard later, they had approached Captain Cleveland, manager of the Hudson's Bay Company's post there, to get news about Knud. The rest of us were of secondary interest.

Captain Cleveland—Sakoatarnak—was quite a person and not without merit. He lived there, the only white man, and his word was law over a district larger than many states in the United States. When we arrived at the station he ordered the natives to cart our belongings from the sledges to his house and to feed our dogs. Then he asked us if there was anything else he could do to please us. We said no, very much impressed by his grandeur. The great man then turned to the natives waiting at the door and, speaking in a soft, mild tone, said: "'Well, then get the hell out of here!"

The Eskimos understood and scuttled away leaving us alone with Cleveland. Knud attempted to explain our arrival and our mission, producing a letter from an officer of the Hudson's Bay Company in London, but Cleveland

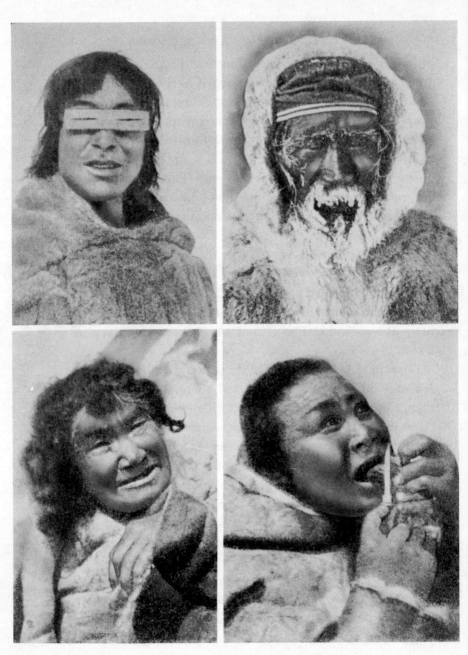

Netchilik Eskimos.

Top: Netchilik women carrying fuel.
Bottom Left: Netchilik woman carrying her child
in her hood.
Bottom Right: Two Netchilik children.

waved it aside: "I don't care to read it. I know good men by sight. I can trust you!"

These were brave words and we were highly flattered. Later we learned that Cleveland could not have read the letter anyhow.

Cleveland was a great character. When we asked him, during our first meal together, whether he would object to our bringing out a bottle of our famous Danish schnapps, he assured us that we could make ourselves at home in his house as long as we desired. "In fact," he assured us, "liquor is my favorite drink—any kind and any brand."

He was limited to six bottles a year "for medical purposes." But, as he was usually ill the very day after the ship arrived with the year's supply, he almost never had any left over for subsequent illnesses.

Cleveland furnished us considerable information about the locality. He had been at Repulse Bay for more than twenty years, first as a whaler (his name Sakoatarnak—The Harpooner—came down from those days). Later he had owned his own ketch with which he had sailed, hunted, traded, and stolen from the natives. After the ketch had been wrecked he became a trader for the Monjo people, fur dealers, until this firm finally was taken over by the Hudson's Bay Company, the largest organization of its kind in the world.

Before the party broke up we were all fast friends.

The Hudson's Bay Company station was transformed by Knud into a place of refuge which we often used. After a while certain misunderstandings arose between him and Captain Cleveland, who thought it quite all right to use us for his own purposes. He raised the prices and tried to dissuade the Eskimos from visiting us. Then Knud reacted in a burst of wrath and went to see him. He wept out his apologies for two days and promised to make amends and to mend his ways. As a token of his friendship, he sent us a sled loaded with gifts of reindeer skins and many other good things, and Knud was prevailed upon to recognize his surrender. Knud's power in the district was firmly established.

One strange thing about Knud Rasmussen was that, while he ordinarily was very fastidious in his habits, on an expedition he was tremendously addicted to smoking. It was all the more remarkable, because in Denmark he was not at all given to smoking. But one of his sore points, which we always teased him about, was that he habitually misplaced his pipe at least twice in every place we stopped or camped. At a given time every evening all skins had to be shaken out and all cooking utensils emptied. He laid his pipe down in the oddest places. There was nothing to be done about it, so we just counted on it.

And it would also affect his spirits to be out of tobacco. We traveled together for fourteen years, but he never learned to take enough tobacco along; and when he did run out he would miss it terribly and begin to complain, and he would get mad at me, who did not smoke, because I didn't seem to care. Every time we left our home I would ask, "Have you got enough tobacco along?" and he always answered that he did, and always he would run out. Experience had therefore taught me to take along a few reserve packages of tobacco, and there would be great joy when I would reach into my sack and bring out a package after a couple of evenings of his complaining and grumbling.

On this expedition, Knud was supposed to gather a collection of amulets and artifacts of all kinds for the museum in Copenhagen. An old spiritualist medium came to us. He was filled with wisdom and burdened with heavy thoughts. But he would not part with his amulets. Then Knud challenged him to take part in a competition.

"I intend to make water burn," said Knud, who poured some white gas on the floor and applied a lighted match so that a big flame roared up. The man was paralyzed with fright.

"And now I'm going to replace air with fire!" cried Knud, and exploded some photography phosphate powder in a big flash.

Then the man gave up.

"No! No!" cried Knud. "I'm not finished!" He grabbed the man by the hand and ran around the house three times with him. The poor man lost his breath with it all.

"And now I propose to let the roof fly off the house if you still think that your spirits are the stronger!"

"Oh, no, no, no!" cried the man. "Rest your powers, and let us remain in here where it is warm. My amulets are poor things and worthless beside yours!" And he then gave up his raven's claw, useful for finding game even in the middle of winter; his stick of wood, which rendered one insensible to pain; his fox tooth, which made one cunning and ingenious; and all the other magical objects that he owned.

In return he received a bottle that had contained salts of ammonia and which gave off a smell that practically tore one's nostrils. Knud tied a string to it and hung it around his neck, and the old man left in a hurry, fearful that Knud would regret the bargain.

There was a man whose name was Kutlok, which means "thumb." He had been on a trip delivering a letter, and this had taken him two years. But he had seen white men, and was therefore an authority in his tribe. When he returned from this postman-trip, he came to our house.

When he departed, he took with him some mementoes of his visit with us, in the form of our tea kettle, some knives, and a dog. He was well on his way before the outraged Eskimos discovered this and told us about it. I decided to pursue him; we could not let a theft go unhindered; but Knud came out of the house and said that he would rather take care of this matter himself. I thought that he should take someone with him, but he didn't want to.

"But at least a weapon to defend yourself with if it comes to a fight?"

He had only a piece of hide to sit on and a whip when his dogs took off. I was not very happy about it.

But Knud Rasmussen had his own methods. What happened between those two I don't know, but late that evening they both returned to the house on their sleds, apparently good friends. They tied their dogs outside the house as usual. Knud came in, and The Thumb came in right behind him, carrying the stolen articles in his hand; he laid them down and with a friendly smile he said, "It seems that a little mistake was made!"

After that he was our friend and we often entrusted him with some of our possessions, leaving them at his house while we were away on journeys.

Then there was a man whose name was Anaqaq. He came from a land far to the west and belonged to a tribe notorious for their filth and squalor. He had never before seen a white man, but he had heard about them. A family quarrel had driven him from his home, which consisted of his wife and her other husband.

So he took to the road, armed only with a salmon spear and a snow knife, and he suffered much hardship by the time he arrived at our house in the company of some of his tribesmen. They were well received and entertained until the end of the four days that we usually housed travelers. Then we told them our hospitality was at an end, and that they ought to be on their way. They left, Anaqaq among them. But after a few days' travel he began to long for Knud, said farewell to his friends, and came back to our house without worrying about whether we wanted to see him or not. He simply told us that our faces were so pleasant to look at that he intended to settle down in our house.

Once again Knud had to perform in his role of arbiter of etiquette. Anaqaq smelled bad enough to more than fill our little house with his stench. But since he was a spiritualist medium and since Knud had quickly discovered that he knew a lot about his tribe's mysticism, we took him on under certain conditions. He was to do everything that he was told, and his catch should belong to us. This last condition he accepted with a sort of indifferent air because, as we soon found out, it didn't amount to much.

After he had been with us for some time, I, who didn't have Knud Rasmussen's patience, became a bit annoyed at him sitting around idle with his hands in his pockets. I gave him some work to do, but got an evasive answer to the effect that he was, after all, a holy man, and that he could on no account be made to do any work. I took it up with Knud and demanded that he discharge him, but Knud did not want to part with his friend.

He called Anaqaq to his room and told him that since they were both holy men they could learn from each other. He said that he had just had a talk with a most powerful helping spirit, who had told him that not only was Anaqaq permitted to work so long as we were there, but, furthermore, it would be highly regarded if he would work as diligently and energetically as possible. Thus buttressed by the supernatural, Anaqaq became active and was really very industrious and helpful.

One evening in "The Bellows," after having worked for days on writing down legends and working with Anaqaq in organizing and presenting the obscure thoughts and words of the local spiritualists, Knud suddenly needed a change and wanted to see some other people. He hitched up his dogs and drove away in the darkness down to a place where some Eskimos lived in their snow huts. The land is very flat there, and when the water is low, the ice breaks up on the rocks, and the only way through it all is very rugged and tortuous. It did no good to whip his dogs. Their harness got caught in the rocks, and their eyes were blinded by the whipping snow blasts they were fighting against. At last Knud lost his patience, and when he reached a drift, he let the dogs lie down as they like to do in a snowstorm, with their tails around their noses, rolled into a ball in order to be snowed under and use the snow as a warming blanket.

Knud, however, had to have shelter. He decided to build himself a snow house. Now fate would have it that on this particular day—undoubtedly for the first time since he had learned to build snow houses—he had forgotten to bring along his snow knife, which is always a necessary tool on a sled journey. He had only a little pocket knife. But since he was never at a loss for a solution, he quickly broke off a slat of wood from a box in which he was carrying some provisions that he wanted to give to the people he was visiting. From this slat he fashioned with his pocket knife a flat, broad knife, and with that he set to work cutting blocks of snow and built himself a modest little house. It took a long time with such a primitive tool, but finally he got it finished, hauled in a couple of furs, and rolled up without eating.

He had no idea that, while quietly lying there, he was in mortal danger. He had not known how close he was to his destination while he was fumbling around in the dark.

Not until morning, when the wind had quieted down and the sun was out, did Knud wake up to a shouting.

"Oh, it is Kununguak's sled, those are Kununguak's dogs!" And he could hear the Eskimos come running down toward his snow house to bid him welcome.

Then they told him that during the night their dogs had gotten the scent of something out on the ice. Some of the men had ventured out to investigate and saw that it was a sled. They also saw, rather hazily, that somebody was building a snow house very close to their houses. They became frightened, because they thought it was a mountain phantom who had camped out there beside their houses, and they decided that it would be best if they were to sneak out and shoot him. If all the men who had guns would line up and shoot at the same time, they thought they would be able to hit him.

But then one of them suggested that maybe this was a

protective spirit who had come to warn them about something—a break in the ice, for instance.

Since the weather was so bad, and it was therefore very unpleasant to go out of doors, they had decided to postpone the shooting until later, and so went to sleep. When they awoke it was light enough to see that it was Kngunguak, as they called Knud.

When we parted after the Hudson's Bay Expedition, Knud Rasmussen and I ended our association in the Arctic exploration field. I returned home, and Knud went on across Canada where he met and studied all the Eskimos who were living in his time.

I visited Alaska eight years after Knud had been there. Old, greasy photographs of Knud were hanging on the walls. Letters which he had written were kept and cherished as relics. Everywhere I was received as a member of the tribe, as a long-awaited friend, only because I had traveled with Knud Rasmussen and was his friend.

Later we went to Greenland together a couple of times, but those were summer trips, and we were both by this time so prosperous that we traveled as passengers on the steamers and had men to work for us, whereas earlier we had done everything ourselves.

But Knud was still Knud. He had received honorary doctorates from two universities, he was covered with medals and honors, and international fame followed in his wake. From all over the world he received offers to take part in expeditions and to participate in the most remarkable undertakings, and still he was the old Knud.

He approached his studies with methods far different

from those that earlier scientific expeditions had used. He first made friends with a people, and got to know their good and their bad points before he made judgments about them, and he never acted in a superior or unapproachable manner. He became one of them and was able to break through their shell of custom and get to the real worth that lay behind. Naturally, he made mistakes, but few people have ever judged others so fairly, and I have never known a man who could forget others' faults so quickly and completely and find compensating good points. This was particularly true in his relations with Eskimos.

And here my recollections about Knud Rasmussen end, but not because everything has been told. A man who, with open eyes and ears, has traveled with Knud Rasmussen for fourteen years could go on and on. The life of one's youth is rich, and it provides experiences and impressions; and in my youth I lived in the same house with Knud Rasmussen, I went on sled journeys with him, and I sat next to him in kayaks. Together we fought ice and current.

No one is born fully formed. Development and education are needed; it is easiest for those who have others to show them the way and to serve as examples. But Knud Rasmussen had no predecessor. He made his own way and a furrow remains behind him, a trail left by his mighty strides through the world. He sometimes told me that he wished he had worked a little harder on his mathematics because his life was such that he often found himself in places where he could have benefited from observations. But to make up for this lack—and I think he was right—he acquired a better relationship with the Eskimos. It would have destroyed their confidence in him and their feeling of equality to see him pull out a theodolite or another magnetic instrument. Instead, he relied on a notebook, in which he wrote down their songs and stories; and a sled, on which he transported the artifacts, clothing, and all the other things that he got from them and which now fill ten halls in the Museum in Copenhagen.

The brisk lad, the affectionate son and brother, the young student who, like Aladdin, accepted the gift of life as a natural right; the resourceful man of action who, with Moltke and Mylius-Erichsen, was the first to forge a path across the ice-bound waters of Melville Bay and so bind Cape York to Denmark; the strong-willed conqueror of snowstorms, cold, and hunger who led his expeditions across Greenland's inland ice to the east coast and the north; the brilliant chief of his own expedition to all of America's Eskimos, an expedition which brought forth the first and only complete study of the Eskimo world's culture and thus made Denmark a model in ethnographic research and spread the fame of our country—all these details go to make up the gigantic personality that was Knud Rasmussen.

I have never met anyone who was able to speak from his inner self and touch his listeners as Knud Rasmussen did in his speeches. When Fridtjof Nansen, his Norwegian peer, died, it was Knud Rasmussen who fully understood what a hero Norway had lost and who eulogized Nansen as the great man of heart and mind that he was; it was a speech that will never be forgotten by those who heard it.

And finally, Knud Rasmussen lived to see a contest between Denmark and Norway before the International Court in The Hague about the rightful possession of

Greenland. Denmark, his beloved fatherland; Norway, his dear and highly regarded Norway, whence his great-grandfather had come to Greenland, where many of his best friends lived, where he had found so many national characteristics and traits he himself valued highly. That these two countries should come to strife was a great sorrow for Knud Rasmussen, and in The Hague he gave a speech— only a few simple words which he uttered because he felt his Eskimo blood in his veins, because he felt himself to be Danish but also felt he had a Norwegian heritage. His point of view was Denmark's, but no one became bitter at his words. They came from a man whose deeds had given him the right to speak, whose incorruptibility was universally recognized, whose mind could not be poisoned by hate, and whose great heart had led him all his life to fight for the Eskimos.

It was a joy for Knud Rasmussen to be able to speak there, and he was gratified that his standpoint was upheld. But Knud Rasmussen could never have said what he said at The Hague with such right and weight if a single chapter of his life had not been lived.

Knud Rasmussen is dead. His casket was surrounded by sorrow, sorrow from all parts of the world. But sorrow was never felt about his deeds, which were clean and unspotted, and I am reminded of a few words of an Eskimo song which he once translated for me, a song about one who had died:

"Like a wanderer's course through the snow was your life.
Your path is marked by a trail, and there are no blots."

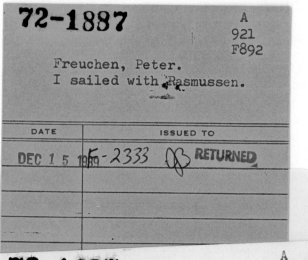